A GASTRONOMIC VADE MECUM

A Gastronomic Vade Mecum

A Christian Field Guide to Eating, Drinking, and Being Merry Now and Forever

John Warwick Montgomery

FIFTEEN · SEVENTEEN PUBLISHING
1517.

A Gastronomic Vade Mecum: A Christian Field Guide to Eating, Drinking and Being Merry Now and Forever
© 2018 John Warwick Montgomery

Published by:
1517 Publishing
PO Box 54032
Irvine, CA 92619-4032

Publisher's Cataloging-In-Publication Data
(Prepared by The Donohue Group, Inc.)

Names: Montgomery, John Warwick.
Title: A gastronomic vade mecum : a Christian field guide to eating, drinking and being merry now and forever / John Warwick Montgomery.
Description: Irvine, CA : 1517 Publishing, [2018]
Identifiers: ISBN 9781945500848 (hardcover) | ISBN 9781945500954 (softcover) | ISBN 9781948969260 (ebook)
Subjects: LCSH: International cooking. | Food—Religious aspects—Christianity. | Dinners and dining—Religious aspects—Christianity. | Fasts and feasts—History. | LCGFT: Cookbooks.
Classification: LCC TX725.A1 M66 2018 (print) | LCC TX725.A1 (ebook) | DDC 641.59—dc23

Printed in the United States of America

Cover design by Brenton Clarke Little

For

Lany Montgomery
Unparalleled apple pie

Jean-Marie Montgomery
*Epitomical barbecues and
consummate salad dressing*

Laurence Montgomery
The best of all possible hachis Parmentier

Primo mirate + deinde gustate + tandem gaudete ad magnam Dei gloriam in unitate sanctorum nostrorum Stephani + Vincentii et Urbani + Amen.

—Grace before meat at the Confrérie Saint-Étienne

* * *

Bless, O Lord, before we dine,
Each dish of food, each cup of wine;
And bless our hearts, that we may be
Aware of what we owe to Thee.

With thankful hearts, O Lord, we ask that we
May never dine without remembering Thee;
And, grateful for our comfortable state,
May leave no Lazarus hungry at the gate.

—Maurice Healy, *Grace Before and After Meat*[1]

---

1 Maurice Healy (1887–1943) was an Irish barrister who wrote both on legal life (*The Old Munster Circuit*) and on ≠wine (*Claret and the White Wines of Bordeaux* and *Stay Me with Flagons*). He was a close friend and disciple of the distinguished gastronome André Simon.

CONTENTS

PREFACE

The Preacher informs us that "of making many books there is no end" (Eccl. 12:12). Culinary titles offer a solid evidence of the truth of this statement. So why another one?

The answer lies in the uniqueness of the present work:

(1) It is the product of far wider scholarship than is usually to be found in its subject area.

(2) Its author has a far wider, more international background than the average writer of culinary treatises.

(3) The book is not beholden to any single restaurant or combination of restaurants for its judgments.

The reader is guaranteed to find here recipes he or she has never encountered before and restaurants at which he or she has never had the privilege of dining.

The volume is also laced with a plethora of historical trivia and amusing asides that will gladden the heart while the reader satisfies the gastronomical urge by consuming dishes prepared from the book's recipes, often translated into English for the first time.

Dr. John Warwick Montgomery
Strasbourg, France
August 10, 2017
The Feast Day of St. Lawrence, Patron of Cooks

Acknowledgments

My thanks to the owners of copyrighted passages included in this work. I have tried assiduously not to exceed the bounds of fair use doctrine in my employment of them.

Much bibliographical assistance has been provided by the following standard works: André L. Simon's introduction in G. Vicaire, *Bibliographie gastronomique*, 2nd ed. (London: Derek Verschoyle, 1954); Catherine Bitting, *Gastronomic Bibliography* (repr., London: Holland Press, 1981); and Gérard Oberlé, *Les fastes de Bacchus et de Comus* (Paris: Editions Belfond, 1989). Useful also is Barbara L. Feret, *Gastronomical and Culinary Literature: A Survey and Analysis of Historically-Oriented Collections in the U.S.A.* (Lanham: Scarecrow Press, 1979).

References to publications in the author's other fields of specialty appear throughout this book. For bibliographical information on them, go to his website: www.jwm.christendom.co.uk. His books are available in the United States from 1517 Legacy: New Reformation Press; titles published in Europe by the Verlag für Kultur und Wissenschaft are distributed in the Americas by Wipf and Stock.

The essay in the introductory section of this book, "Transcendental Gastronomy," can also be found in my work *Christ as Centre and Circumference*. "A Vinific Critique of Bad Biblical Criticism" appears as well in *Defending the*

Gospel in Legal Style. "Preferences—from the Author's Autobiography" is extracted from an appendix to *Fighting the Good Fight: A Life in Defense of the Faith.*

INTRODUCTION

1 | Fundamental Culinary Principles

20 + 3 Culinary Axioms

1. Never eat junk food; it will deaden your palate so that you will not appreciate great cuisine.
2. Do not smoke; you will so dull your palate that you might as well eat the tablecloth as what is served on it.
3. Ladies, never wear a heavy perfume to a fine dinner; if you do, the diners will be sensing you rather than, or in combination with, the food and wine.
4. Realize that dining is a total experience: the atmosphere and the setting must be ideal, not just the food and the service.
5. French cuisine is the apogee; next comes the Chinese.
6. The less the consumer or guest has to do, the better the experience; avoid culinary situations where one must engage in cutting or heating food oneself. (Exception: barbecues, but even there, less is more.)
7. Strangely shaped dishware should be avoided; the flatter the dish (the medieval "trencher"), the easier to manage.

8. Never accept colored dishware or dishware with odd designs, since they divert attention from the food. (But gold dessert ware is a very nice touch.)

9. Do not worry about the political correctness of what you eat; *rognons de veau* (veal kidneys) may not sound like a good conversation piece, but they can be a wonderful treat.

10. Contrasting but complementary tastes are vital (thus, as a simple example, anchovies or parmesan cheese in a lettuce salad).

11. Sauces, seldom featured in American cuisine and largely avoided by the primitive British, are of utmost importance; they must precisely conjoin with the food in which they are used. Thus a St. Pierre fish dish requires a stronger sauce than one would normally use with fish (perhaps even a *sauce béarnaise?*).

12. Full-bodied wines should accompany strong foods; light wines should be served with light foods. Thus the normal practice is red wine with meat (heavier Bordeaux reds with game, less full-bodied Beaujolais reds with duck) and white wines with fish, chicken, or light salads.

Expressed as a continuum:
Substantial dish >>>>>>>>>>>>>>>> Lighter dish
Red wine >>>>>>>>>>>>>>>>>>>>>>>> White wine

Note that the issue is not really "red" vs. "white": it is the degree of strength/fullness of the body of the wine in question. Thus the white Alsatian muscat can go splendidly with a meat dish.

13. Rose wines, with the exception of the Alsatian Pinot Noir (really a light red), like the rather happy-go-lucky Mediterranean areas from which they generally come, are neither fish nor fowl. They are said to go with everything, but they therefore really go with nothing and should be consumed in hot summer weather for fun, not for culinary appreciation.

14. Dry wines are definitely preferable to sweet wines (beloved by the Germans, sadly), since a sweet wine will almost invariably overwhelm the food with which it is consumed. In general, restrict yourself to sweet wines with desserts. (An exception: the Alsatian *Gewürztraminer* is perfect with the greatest of all culinary delicacies, *pâté de foie gras d'oie*—goose liver pate.)

15. Champagnes are generally overrated; they are brittle and a bit like aristocratic ladies who look down on you and will not give you the time of day. Consider the *crémants*—the regional productions employing the champagne process but with local grapes—such as a Crémant d'Alsace made from the Pinot Blanc. They will be much less expensive and display a more interesting taste quality. Avoid at all costs "sparkling wine" (the product of carbonization, not the *méthode champenoise*).

16. As for restaurants, seek those where the service is unpretentious but impeccable (e.g., unobtrusive waiters/waitresses who are aware of your every need and do not need to be signaled by the customers).

17. In a good restaurant, do not fear to order wine *en pichet*; in a questionable restaurant, always order wine by the bottle.

18. Culinary guides, such as those published by Michelin, are of value chiefly because they will reduce chances of a poor meal. They do not, however, list many wonderful restaurants at much more reasonable prices; these you must discover for yourself. The three-star Michelin restaurants often receive that rating as a result of wild culinary speculations (e.g., *filet de tigre*—that is a joke, of course, but the reality may be no better and, in any event, astronomically expensive).

19. A meal is a symphony: it should begin simply (the *entrée*), rise steadily to a crescendo (the *plat*), and end with comforting harmony (*fromage et dessert*).

20. Life is short and the number of meals finite; one must therefore insist on quality and refuse compromise.

Theological Reflections (a Trinitarian Three)

1. Banquets are central in both the Old and New Testaments.

2. The Lord's Supper is one of only two sacraments universally recognized by all Christian churches.

3. The "Marriage Supper of the Lamb" (Rev. 19) requires a proper wedding garment (Matt. 22)—namely, Christ's righteousness—obtained by faith in His death for our sins and resurrection for our justification. *Whatever you do, do not miss this banquet at the end of time!*

2 | Transcendental Gastronomy

The holiday season is nearly upon us: Thanksgiving, soon to be followed by Christmas. Times of merriment, good fellowship, and banqueting—and times, for many evangelicals, of guilt-ridden, conscience-stricken breast-beating. How can we kill the fatted calf (even if we can still afford the inflationary beast) when others less fortunate do not have one? Should we not instead try to get by on the barest minimum in protest against the consumerist society and its values? One West Coast evangelical couple has recently written on behalf of "Christian poverty," describing the humble, sanctified growing of their own vegetables (and their own attempt at making toothpaste, which, however, proved abrasive to the teeth).

Ambivalently torn by competing values, evangelicals realize dimly that they cannot reject the season's festal board without contributing to the demise of holidays that are essentially or should be holy days; yet their Protestant work ethic and a somber strain of pietism cast a dark cloud of self-doubt over the candlelit table.

On November 13, 1974, in Paris, I had the temerity to accept the invitation of the French Gastronomical

Academy to become one of its fifty living academicians and occupy the chair named for Bertrand Guégan, the translator of *Apicius* and author of several classic works on cuisine. During the previous summer, I had conducted two seminars on gastronomy in Strasbourg for the benefit of overflow audiences concerned with the significance of cuisine. Another sign of my hopelessly unsanctified state? Possibly, but bear with me; even Balaam's ass—an eater of straw—had something to say.

I am convinced that evangelicals (whom some clever critic has called "the monks of Protestantism") have so allowed their negative attitude toward "the world" to influence them that in the realm of eating, as in so many other realms (such as entertainment, dress, art, and literature), they cut themselves off from God's creative gifts. I believe, contra more than one evangelical, that gastronomy is not to be classed among the materialistic "lower immediacies" at the bottom of the axiological ladder of values (to use the expression of the late Edward John Carnell of Fuller Seminary in his *Philosophy of the Christian Religion*), but deserves transcendental status! In the words of the greatest of all writers on the subject, Brillat-Savarin (*The Physiology of Taste*), gourmandism, far from representing the deadly sin of gluttony—which arises from its *misuse*—"denotes implicit obedience to the commands of the Creator, who bade us eat that we might live."

But here we must be careful, as with all discussion of the transcendental. Metaphysical speculations apart from revelation have been trivial at best, pompous at worst—mercifully relieved only by unconscious humor. The dangers relative to gastronomical speculation are hilariously set out in Marcel Rouff's classic *The Life and Passion of Dodin-Bouffant, Gourmet*, where the hero, on a visit to Germany, encounters "Prof. Dokt. Hugo Stumm," a philosopher who has already churned out the first 1,783 pages of his definitive Hegelian-Platonic masterpiece, "The Metaphysics of Cuisine," and who, in order practically to reflect the transcendental purity of food as an Ideal, now eats nothing but boiled potatoes and cauliflower!

In this matter, as in all others that touch eternity, only scriptural revelation can keep us from speculative absurdity. But here many evangelicals are in for a surprise, for our sociological pietism has blinded us to a powerful biblical emphasis. Throughout Scripture, eating and drinking are regularly associated with events of the highest theological and spiritual importance.

The Bible opens with man's fall—described in terms of choosing to eat not what God had provided but what he had forbidden ("Of every tree of the garden thou mayest freely eat, but of the tree of the knowledge of good and evil"); it ends with the Marriage Supper of the Lamb, eschatologically restoring Eden and ushering in the New Heaven and New Earth (Rev. 19:9). The prime representation of grace under the Old Covenant was the Passover meal, and it foreshadowed the Sacrament of Eucharist, which our Lord expressly connects with the eternal Marriage Supper when he says, "I will not drink henceforth of this fruit of the vine until that day when I drink it new with you in my Father's kingdom" (Matt. 26:29 and parallels). The centrality of feasting in the early church is evidenced by its agapae, or love feasts, and the observance of the "feasts" or "festivals" of the saints has been a vital part of Christian worship in all the historic confessional traditions.

The conclusion seems inescapable that the Lord of Scripture wants our meals—as the most basic and regular of our conscious activities—to remind us of things eternal. To be sure, our table graces are a halting recognition of this, but do we exercise our talents to prepare meals artistically and gastronomically worthy of the graces we say over them?

The Alsatian Confrérie Saint-Étienne uses the invitatory "Primo mirate, deinde gustate, tandem gaudete ad magnam Dei gloriam" (First look with wonder, then taste, finally give praise to God's great glory). How many of our meals compel us to look with wonder and taste with praise? Could our reliance on TV dinners signify just the opposite of spirituality—a gross indifference to and ingratitude for God's culinary gifts to us? As Brillat-Savarin aphoristically and uncomfortably put it, "Tell me what you eat: I will tell you what you are."

This holiday season, is it not time to apply Horatius Bonar's Communion hymn in its widest sense?

Feast after feast thus comes and passes by,
Yet, passing, points to the glad feast above,

Giving sweet foretaste of the festal joy,
The Lamb's great bridal feast of bliss and love.

Sociologist Peter Berger, in his *Rumor of Angels*, notes that certain activities—from children's games to great concerts—can link one to eternity, for as one is caught up in them, time and mortality seem momentarily arrested and a window opens to another world. Banquets and feasts can be like that. If you listen very closely at your Thanksgiving or Christmas table, you may just hear the flutter of angels' wings: a cloud of witnesses rejoicing with you, waiting to welcome you to an even greater banquet.

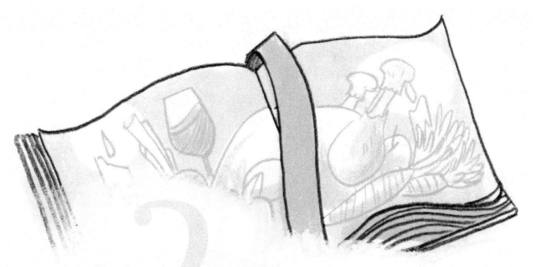

FOOD AS LITERATURE
Tasty Selections

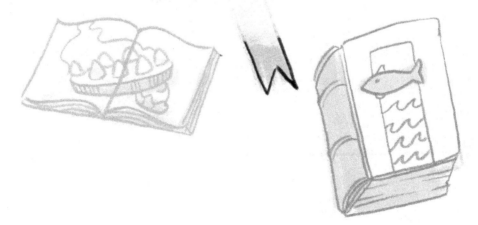

1 | Biblical Perspective

The dietary laws of the Old Testament are often incomprehensible to modern people. In point of fact, they were of the utmost importance in preserving the Jewish nation from plague and illness, creating a united people, and fostering holiness—so as to keep that chosen people intact for the coming of the Messiah. (See, even with its limitations, C. Raimer Smith, *The Physician Examines the Bible* [New York: Philosophical Library, 1950].)

The fact that no reason is given for some of these Old Testament prohibitions is no argument against them. If they were of divine origin, violating them would be *lèse majesté* in any event, as with the command in the Garden of Eden not to eat the fruit of a certain tree, even though nothing was said as to why that particular tree should be avoided and not others.

After the coming of the Messiah and the beginning of the New Covenant, the Jewish dietary restrictions lost their force (Acts 10; Col. 2:16; 1 Cor. 10:30–31; 1 Tim. 4:1–5).

As for our Lord Himself, His mission was that that of *salvation*: as the angel announced to Joseph, "You shall call his name Jesus, for he shall save his people from their sins" (Matt. 1:21; cf. John 20:31). But it is clear that Jesus would have accepted the fundamental axiom of the culinary arts:

quality (Culinary Principle 20). Concerning food, Jesus used the analogy of *good* and *bad* salt: "Salt is good, but if it loses its savour it is good for nothing but to be cast out" (Matt. 5:13; Luke 14:34). And as for drink, Jesus made sure that water was turned into *good* wine: "When the master of the feast tasted the water now become wine, and did not know where it came from (though the servants who had drawn the water knew), the master of the feast called the bridegroom and said to him, 'Everyone serves the good wine first, and when people have drunk freely, then the poor wine. But you have kept the good wine until now'" (John 2; and see "A Vinific Critique of Bad Biblical Criticism" in the appendices of this book).

The early church regularly conducted "agape" feasts. The word is a unique New Testament usage to make clear that Christian love was neither the practice of simple friendship (i.e., *filia*—cf. Philadelphia, the "City of Brotherly Love") nor a using of others to satisfy one's needs and desires (i.e., *eros*), but the love of God that saves the unworthy, creating a model for believers to serve their neighbors. See V. Ermoni, *L'Agapé dans l'Église primitive* (Paris: Librairie Bloud, 1906); and Anders Nygren, *Agape and Eros* (Philadelphia: Westminster Press, 1953).

The observant reader will note that our discussion here connects with the "Theological Reflections" following our "Fundamental Culinary Principals" (part 1, *infra*).

2 | Martin Luther and His Wife, Katherine von Bora

Roland H. Bainton, in *Here I Stand*, his classic biography of the Reformer, correctly maintains than if you try to understand the Protestant Reformation as anything other than a *theological movement*, you will never understand it. It cannot be reduced to politics, economics, sociology—or cuisine.

But Martin Luther had high regard for good food and good drink, and by God's grace, he was provided with a wife who maintained such standards.

Here are some statements from the Reformer followed by accounts relating to his wife, Katherine.

Luther

We are to lead a spiritual life, but in such a way that also the body may enjoy its recreation. This principle applies particularly to those who do hard work or suffer great temptations and are troubled with sleeplessness. These may drink more freely in order to quiet themselves and induce sleep. That is why Holy Scripture says [Psalm 104:15] wine was created in order to make glad the sad and afflicted heart of man. Such a person should eat and drink in order to bring body and soul together again.

So we are to go on our way down the royal middle, turning neither into Epicureans and dissolute sots nor into sad monks and hypocrites. . . .

God hates sadness and loves a joyful and honest heart; for enough are the troubles and the sadness which the devil inflicts on men in other respects. Therefore the body is to be accorded its honour and care, but not to the point of making it wanton and indulging it in all sorts of shameful excesses. (*WA* 43,334)

* * *

Once when he was drinking some excellent wine, he [Luther] said, "I don't believe our Lord God will ever give more than he has given to the peasants. He gives them such good wine, grain, eggs, chickens, etc. Indeed, he gives them all created things. . . . From the fact that he bestows such great gifts on the wicked and those who blaspheme him, we can conclude what he will give us." (*Table Talk*, no. 443, early in 1533)

[Author note: It is a fundamental principle of Luther scholarship that *Table Talk* recordings must never be cited against what Luther says in his own writings. Why? There is always the possibility that, as notes were being taken at table by those eating with the Luthers in the Black Cloister, someone belched or had an attack of the hiccups, thereby obscuring or distorting what Luther was actually saying.]

Katherine von Bora

Several books devoted to the former nun and devoted wife of the Reformer have been published. They are not very satisfactory—being either agonizingly hagiographical or (more recently) attempts to show that Katherine von Bora was a model of the modern, liberated woman. The best treatment is a short, but fully documented, article by Roland H. Bainton that can be found in his book *Women of the Reformation in Germany and Italy* (Minneapolis: Augsburg, 1971); the material to follow comes from that article.

As an aside, when I was chairman of the Department of Church History at the Trinity Evangelical Divinity School, I invited Bainton to come from Yale to deliver guest lectures there. Unfortunately, he learned that I am bilingual (French and English). During the weekend at the divinity school, he insisted on speaking with me only in French. This was sheer agony, since his knowledge of written French was accompanied by a perfectly terrible French pronunciation—and, as his host, I had to grin and bear it.

* * *

Katherine ministered to her husband's diseases, depressions, and eccentricities. She had great skill with diet, herbs, poultices, and massages. Her son, later a distinguished physician [see my work "The Life of Paul Luther, Physician," in *Christ as Centre and Circumference*] praised her as half a doctor. Luther frequently suffered tortures from the stone. On one such occasion he would neither eat nor drink, and Katie besought him to take some sustenance. "Very well," said he, "roast beef, peas, and mustard and be quick before my fancy fades." She complied and he ate heartily. His doctors called and were aghast. They returned in the morning to see the corpse and found him at his desk. He had passed a stone.

* * *

Letter of Luther to his wife, July 29, 1534: "Grace and peace in Christ, dear Lord Katie! Yesterday, I had a good drink. I thought of what good wine and beer I have at home and a lovely wife, or should I say lord? You'd do well to send me our whole cellar full of wine and a flask of your beer as soon as you can. I commend you to God with all the young ones and relatives. *Dein liebchen . . .*"

3 | Anthelme Brillat-Savarin

This nineteenth-century French magistrate is the undisputed master philosopher of the culinary art. His great work *La Physiologie du goût* (*The Physiology of Taste*) was first published in 1825 and has been translated into English several times, the most authoritative English edition being that by M. F. K. Fisher (Berkeley, CA: North Point Press, 1986). Other editions have appeared with the title *The Philosopher in the Kitchen*. For background on Brillat-Savarin, I suggest Thierry Boissel's *Brillat-Savarin (1755–1826), un chevalier candide* (Paris: Presses de la Renaissance, 1989) and Giles MacDonogh's *Brillat-Savarin: The Judge and His Stomach* (London: John Murray, 1992).

Why Salvador Dali would have characterized Brillat-Savarin as a "positivist-materialist" is beyond my comprehension—except, of course, for Dali's own bizarre "Catholic" mysticism (*Les Dîners de Gala*, trans. J. Peter Moore [Cologne, Germany: Taschen, 2016]; cf. Dali's *The Wines of Gala*, trans. Olivier Bernier [New York: Harry N. Abrams, 1978]).

I reproduce in translation from *The Physiology of Taste* Brillat-Savarin's fundamental axioms, suggesting that the reader compare them with his or her own.

Aphorisms of the Professor
To Serve as Prolegomena to His Work
and Eternal Basis to the Science.

    I. The universe would be nothing were it not for life, and all that lives must be fed.

    II. Animals fill themselves; man eats. The man of mind alone knows how to eat.

    III. The destiny of nations depends on the manner in which they are fed.

    IV. Tell me what kind of food you eat, and I will tell you what kind of person you are.

    V. The Creator, when he obliges man to eat, invites him to do so by appetite and rewards him by pleasure.

    VI. Gourmandise is an act of judgment, in obedience to which we grant a preference to things that are agreeable over those that have not that quality.

    VII. The pleasure of the table belongs to all ages, to all conditions, to all countries, and to all eras; it mingles with all other pleasures and remains at the last to console us for their departure.

    VIII. The table is the only place where one does not suffer from boredom during the first hour.

IX. The discovery of a new dish confers more happiness on humanity than the discovery of a new star.

X. Those persons who suffer from indigestion, or who become drunk, are utterly ignorant of the true principles of eating and drinking.

XI. The order of food is from the most substantial to the lightest.

XII. The order of drinking is from the mildest to the headiest and most aromatic.

XIII. To say that we should not vary our wines is a heresy; the tongue can react dully even to the best bottle after the third glass from it.

XIV. A dessert without cheese is like a beautiful woman with only one eye.

XV. A cook may be taught, but a man who can roast is born with that faculty.

XVI. The most indispensable quality of a good cook is promptness. It should also be that of his guests.

XVII. To wait too long for a dilatory guest shows disrespect to those who are punctual.

XVIII. He who receives friends and pays no attention to the repast prepared for them is not fit to have friends.

XIX. The mistress of the house should always be certain that the coffee is excellent, the master that his liquors are of the first quality.

XX. To invite a person to your house is to take charge of his happiness as long as he is beneath your roof.

4 | Anthony Trollope

It is said that in France, breakfast is nothing and the other meals are everything, whereas in England, breakfast is everything and the rest of the meals are best forgotten. I do not pronounce on the truth of this aphorism, but I do provide Victorian novelist Anthony Trollope's mouth-watering description of breakfast at Plumstead Episcopi (from *The Warden* [1855; repr., London: Penguin Books, 1994]).

* * *

The tea consumed was the very best, the coffee the very blackest, the cream the very thickest; there was dry toast and buttered toast, muffins and crumpets; hot bread and cold bread, white bread and brown bread, home-made bread and bakers' bread, wheaten bread and oaten bread; and if there be other breads than these, they were there; there were eggs in napkins, and crispy bits of bacon under silver covers; and there were little fishes in a little box, and devilled kidneys frizzling on a hot-water dish; which, by-the-by, were placed closely contiguous to the plate of the worthy archdeacon himself. Over and above this, on a snow-white napkin, spread upon the sideboard, was a huge ham and a huge sirloin; the latter having laden the dinner table on the previous evening. Such was the culinary fare at Plumstead Episcopi.

5 | Dining at the Athenaeum

My London club is the Athenaeum, once a men's club, now open also to the distaff side of mankind. Membership is a long and tedious process, since one does not only have to be nominated by a member, but the nomination has to be subsequently reinforced with the signatures of a dozen other members. Blackballing is always possible.

The history of the club is replete with fascinating occurrences. After refusing to speak to each other for three years, Charles Dickens and William Makepeace Thackeray, both members, reconciled at the foot of the majestic staircase leading to the library. The club has welcomed a host of Nobel Prize winners into membership.

Here is a short description of the club, from Robin McDouall's *Clubland Cooking* (London: Phaidon Press, 1974):

The Athenaeum [was] built by Decimus Burton in 1829. The frivolous, the social, the political and the gamblers had been provided for at White's, Brooks's, Boodle's, Almack's. The Athenaeum, originally called "The Society" was for the intellectuals. Sir Humphrey Davy, Sir Francis Chantry, Sir Thomas Lawrence, Sir Walter Scott, Thomas Moore were among the founders. Even now, you can hardly put a pin between bishops and, if you do, you will probably impale a nuclear physicist. It has the reputation of having the best library of any club in London. Its cellar, too, has a high reputation. Rather unfairly, from Victorian times until today it has a poor reputation for its food. I can't think why. When my old friend Maurice Hastings was alive, we used to have the finest oysters and *tournedos* washed down by vast quantities of Louis Roederer. If guests complain of the food there, it must, I think, be because they are entertained by underpaid suffragan bishops: I have always done very well.

A nineteenth-century reinforcement of McDouall's positive take on the Athenaeum dining experience is the following (from *The Epicure's Year Book and Table Companion,* ed. William Blanchard Jerrold [London: Bradbury, 1869]):

A friend of mine called to propose that we should dine together at the Athenaeum, and he would send a brace of grouse he had received. We dined very satisfactorily but agreed that a perfect edition of our dinner would have been as follows:—

First, a dozen and half of small oysters, not pampered, but fresh from their native bed, eaten simply after the French fashion, with lemon juice, to give an edge to the appetite. In about twenty minutes, the time for dressing them, three fine flounders water-zoutchied [= stewed, with just enough liquid to cover them], with brown bread and butter—a dish that is better served at The Athenaeum than anywhere I know. At a short interval after the flounders, the grouse, not sent up together, but one after the other, hot and hot, like mutton chops, each accompanied by a plate of French beans. With the flounders, half a pint of sherry, and with the grouse a bottle of genuine claret, which we get for three-and-sixpence a bottle [!!]; after which, a cup each of strong hot coffee.

6 | Alphonse Daudet

Alphonse Daudet (1840–1897) was one of the most prolific and widely read French novelists of the nineteenth century. His most celebrated books were *Lettres de mon moulin* and *Tartarin de Tarascon*. Here *in toto* is his "The Three Low Masses: A Christmas Story," one of the tales comprising *Lettres de mon moulin*. It nicely sets fine cuisine over against the perennial temptation of gluttony and shows the great danger of substituting lower pleasures for higher things (cf. Edward John Carnell, *A Philosophy of the Christian Religion*).

Léon Daudet (1867–1942), son of Alphonse, who was a writer and journalist and a strong monarchist like his father, appreciated fine food and wrote most attractively on the subject. See his essays "Réhabilitation de l'Ail" in *Gastronomie* ("Les Cahiers de la République des Lettres, des Sciences et des Arts," 2ème année, no. 9 [Paris: Les Beaux Arts, 1927]) and "À Table, ou les plaisirs de la gourmandise" in *Plaisirs* (ed. Roger Dacosta [Paris: Laboratoire de l'Hépatrol, 1934]), containing his mouth-watering account of an Alsatian repast.

* * *

I

"Two truffled turkeys, Garrigou?"

"Yes, your reverence, two magnificent turkeys, stuffed with truffles. I should know something about it, for I myself helped to fill them. One would have said their skin would crack as they were roasting, it is that stretched . . ."

"Jesu-Maria! I who like truffles so much! . . . Quick, give me my surplice, Garrigou. . . . And have you seen anything else in the kitchen besides the turkeys?"

"Yes, all kinds of good things. . . . Since noon, we have done nothing but pluck pheasants, hoopoes, barn-fowls, and woodcocks. Feathers were flying about all over. . . . Then they have brought eels, gold carp, and trout out of the pond, besides . . ."

"What size were the trout, Garrigou?"

"As big as that, your reverence. . . . Enormous!"

"Oh heavens! I think I see them. . . . Have you put the wine in the vessels?"

"Yes, your reverence, I have put the wine in the vessels. . . . But la! it is not to be compared to what you will drink presently, when the midnight mass is over. If you only saw that in the dining hall of the château! The decanters are all full of wines glowing with every colour! . . . And the silver plate, the chased *epergnes*, the flowers, the lustres! . . . Never will such another midnight repast be seen. The noble marquis has invited all the lords of the neighbourhood. At least forty of you will sit down to table, without reckoning the farm bailiff and the notary. . . . Oh, how lucky is your reverence to be one of them! . . . After a mere sniff of those fine turkeys, the scent of truffles follows me everywhere. . . . Yum!"

"Come now, come now, my child. Let us keep from the sin of gluttony, on the night of the Nativity especially. . . . Be quick and light the wax-tapers and ring the first bell for the mass; for it's nearly midnight and we must not be behind time."

This conversation took place on a Christmas night in the year of grace one thousand six hundred and something, between the Reverend Dom Balaguère (formerly Prior of the Barnabites, now paid chaplain of the Lords of Trinquelague), and his little clerk Garrigou, or at least him whom he took for his little clerk Garrigou, for you must know that the devil had on that night assumed the round face and soft features of the young sacristan, in order the more effectually to lead the reverend father into temptation, and make him commit the dreadful sin of gluttony. Well then, while the supposed Garrigou (hum!) was with all his might making the bells of the baronial chapel chime out, his reverence was putting on his chasuble in the little sacristy of the château; and with his mind already agitated by all these gastronomic descriptions, he kept saying to himself as he was robing:

"Roasted turkeys, . . . golden carp, . . . trout as big as that! . . ."

Out of doors, the soughing night wind was carrying abroad the music of the bells, and with this, lights began to make their appearance on the dark sides of Mount Ventoux, on the summit of which rose the ancient towers of Trinquelague. The lights were borne by the families of the tenant farmers, who were coming to hear the midnight mass at the château. They were scaling the hill in groups of five or six together, and singing; the father in front carrying a lantern, and the women wrapped up in large brown cloaks, beneath which their little children snuggled and sheltered. In spite of the cold and the lateness of the hour these good folks were marching blithely along, cheered by the thought that after the mass was over there would be, as always in former years, tables set for them down in the kitchens. Occasionally the glass windows in some lord's carriage, preceded by torch-bearers, would glisten in the moon-light on the rough ascent; or perhaps a mule would jog by with tinkling bells, and by the light of the misty lanterns the tenants would recognize their bailiff and would salute him as he passed with:

"Good evening, Master Arnoton."

"Good evening. Good evening, my friend."

The night was clear, and the stars were twinkling with frost; the north wind was nipping, and at times a fine small hail, that slipped off one's garments without wetting them, faithfully maintained the tradition of Christmas being white with snow. On the summit of the hill, as the goal towards which all were wending, gleamed the château, with its enormous mass of towers and gables, and its chapel steeple rising into the blue-black sky. A multitude of little lights were twinkling, coming, going, and moving about at all the windows; they looked like the sparks one sees running about in the ashes of burnt paper.

After you had passed the drawbridge and the postern gate, it was necessary, in order to reach the chapel, to cross the first court, which was full of carriages, foot-men and sedan chairs, and was quite illuminated by the blaze of torches and the glare of the kitchen fires. Here were heard the click of turnspits, the rattle of sauce-pans, the clash of glasses and silver plate in the commotion attending the preparation of the feast; while over all rose a warm vapour smelling pleasantly of roast meat, piquant herbs, and complex sauces, and which seemed to say to the farmers, as well as to the chaplain and to the bailiff, and to everybody:

"What a good midnight repast we are going to have after the mass!"

II

Ting-a-ring!—a—ring!

The midnight mass is beginning in the chapel of the château, which is a cathedral in miniature, with groined and vaulted roofs, oak wood-work as high as the walls, expanded draperies, and tapers all aglow. And what a lot of people! What grand dresses! First of all, seated in

the carved stalls that line the choir, is the Lord of Trinquelague in a coat of salmon-coloured silk, and about him
are ranged all the noble lords who have been invited.

On the opposite side, on velvet-covered praying-stools,
the old dowager marchioness in flame-coloured brocade, and the youthful Lady of Trinquelague wearing a
lofty head-dress of plaited lace in the newest fashion of
the French court, have taken their places. Lower down,
dressed in black, with punctilious wigs, and shaven
faces, like two grave notes among the gay silks and the
figured damasks, are seen the bailiff, Thomas Arnoton,
and the notary Master Ambroy. Then come the stout
major-domos, the pages, the horsemen, the stewards,
Dame Barbara, with all her keys hanging at her side on
a real silver ring. At the end, on the forms, are the lower
class, the female servants, the cotter farmers and their
families; and lastly, down there, near the door, which they
open and shut very carefully, are messieurs the scullions,
who enter in the interval between two sauces, to take a
little whiff of mass; and these bring the smell of the repast
with them into the church, which now is in high festival
and warm from the number of lighted tapers.

Is it the sight of their little white caps that so distracts
the celebrant? Is it not rather Garrigou's bell? that mad
little bell which is shaken at the altar foot with an infernal
impetuosity that seems all the time to be saying: "Come,
let us make haste, make haste. . . . The sooner we shall
have finished, the sooner shall we be at table." The fact

is that every time this devil's bell tinkles the chaplain forgets his mass, and thinks of nothing but the midnight repast. He fancies he sees the cooks bustling about, the stoves glowing with forge-like fires, the two magnificent turkeys, filled, crammed, marbled with truffles. . . .

Then again he sees, passing along, files of little pages carrying dishes enveloped in tempting vapours, and with them he enters the great hall now prepared for the feast. Oh delight! there is the immense table all laden and luminous, peacocks adorned with their feathers, pheasants spreading out their reddish-brown wings, ruby-coloured decanters, pyramids of fruit glowing amid green boughs, and those wonderful fish Garrigou (ah well, yes, Garrigou!) had mentioned, laid on a couch of fennel, with their pearly scales gleaming as if they had just come out of the water, and bunches of sweet-smelling herbs in their monstrous snouts. So clear is the vision of these marvels that it seems to Dom Balaguère that all these wondrous dishes are served before him on the embroidered altar-cloth, and two or three times instead of the *Dominus vobiscum*, he finds himself saying the *Benedicite*. Except these slight mistakes, the worthy man pronounces the service very conscientiously, without skipping a line, without omitting a genuflexion; and all goes tolerably well until the end of the first mass; for you know that on Christmas Day the same officiating priest must celebrate three consecutive masses.

"That's one done!" says the chaplain to himself with a sigh of relief; then, without losing a moment, he motioned to his clerk, or to him whom he supposed to be his clerk, and . . .

"Ting-a-ring . . . Ting-a-ring, a-ring!"

Now the second mass is beginning, and with it begins also Dom Balaguère's sin. "Quick, quick, let us make haste," Garrigou's bell cries out to him in its shrill little voice, and this time the unhappy celebrant, completely given over to the demon of gluttony, fastens upon the missal and devours its pages with the eagerness of his over-excited appetite. Frantically he bows down, rises up, merely indicates the sign of the cross and the genuflexions, and curtails all his gestures in order to get sooner finished. Scarcely has he stretched out his arms at the gospel, before he is striking his breast at the *Confiteor*. It is a contest between himself and the clerk as to who shall mumble the faster. Versicles and responses are hurried over and run one into another. The words, half pronounced, without opening the mouth, which would take up too much time, terminate in unmeaning murmurs.

"*Oremus ps . . . ps . . . ps . . .*"

"*Mea culpa . . . pa . . . pa . . .*"

Like vintagers in a hurry pressing grapes in the vat, these two paddle in the mass Latin, sending splashes in every direction.

"*Dom . . . scum! . . .*" says Balaguère.

". . . *Stutuo! . . .*" replies Garrigou; and all the time the cursed little bell is tinkling there in their ears, like the jingles they put on post-horses to make them gallop fast. You may imagine at that speed a low mass is quickly disposed of.

"That makes two," says the chaplain quite panting; then without taking time to breathe, red and perspiring, he descends the altar steps and . . .

"Ting-a-ring! . . . Ting-a-ring! . . ."

Now the third mass is beginning. There are but a few more steps to be taken to reach the dining-hall; but, alas! the nearer the midnight repast approaches the more does the unfortunate Balaguère feel himself possessed by mad impatience and gluttony. The vision becomes more distinct; the golden carps, the roasted turkeys are there, there! . . . He touches them, . . . he . . . oh heavens! The dishes are smoking, the wines perfume the air; and with furiously agitated clapper, the little bell is crying out to him:

"Quick, quick, quicker yet!"

But how could he go quicker? His lips scarcely move. He no longer pronounces the words; . . . unless he were to impose upon Heaven outright and trick it out of its mass. . . . And that is precisely what he does, the unfortunate man! . . . From temptation to temptation; he begins by skipping a verse, then two. Then the epistle is too long—he does not finish it, skims over the gospel, passes before the *Credo* without going into it, skips the *Pater*, salutes the *Preface* from a distance, and by leaps and bounds thus hurls himself into eternal damnation, constantly followed by the vile Garrigou (*vade retro, Satanas!*), who seconds him with wonderful skill, sustains his chasuble, turns over the leaves two at a time, elbows the reading-desks, upsets the vessels, and is continually sounding the little bell louder and louder, quicker and quicker.

You should have seen the scared faces of all who were present, as they were obliged to follow this mass by mere mimicry of the priest, without hearing a word; some rise when others kneel, and sit down when the others are standing up, and all the phases of this singular service are mixed up together in the multitude of different attitudes presented by the worshippers on the benches . . .

"The *abbé* goes too fast. . . . One can't follow him," murmured the old dowager, shaking her head-dress in confusion. Master Arnoton with great steel spectacles on his nose is searching in his prayer-book to find where the dickens they are. But at heart all these good folks, who themselves are thinking about feasting, are not sorry that the mass is going on at this post haste; and when Dom Balaguère with radiant face turns towards those present and cries with all his might: "*Ite, missa est*," they all respond to him a "*Deo gratias*" in but one voice, and that as joyous and enthusiastic, as if they thought themselves already seated at the midnight repast and drinking the first toast.

III
Five minutes afterwards the crowd of nobles were sitting down in the great hall, with the chaplain in the midst of

them. The château, illuminated from top to bottom, was resounding with songs, with shouts, with laughter, with uproar; and the venerable Dom Balaguère was thrusting his fork into the wing of a fowl, and drowning all remorse for his sin in streams of regal wine and the luscious juices of the viands. He ate and drank so much, the dear, holy man, that he died during the night of a terrible attack, without even having had time to repent; and then in the morning when he got to heaven, I leave you to imagine how he was received.

He was told to withdraw on account of his wickedness. His fault was so grievous that it effaced a whole lifetime of virtue. . . . He had robbed them of a midnight mass. . . . He should have to pay for it with three hundred, and he should not enter into Paradise until he had celebrated in his own chapel these three hundred Christmas masses in the presence of all those who had sinned with him and by his fault. . . .

. . . And now this is the true legend of Dom Balaguère as it is related in the olive country. At the present time the château of Trinquelague no longer exists, but the chapel still stands on the top of Mount Ventoux, amid a cluster of green oaks. Its decayed door rattles in the wind, and its threshold is choked up with vegetation; there are birds' nests at the corners of the altar, and in the recesses of the lofty windows, from which the stained glass has long ago disappeared. It seems, however, that every year at Christmas, a supernatural light wanders amid these ruins, and the peasants, in going to the masses and to the midnight repasts, see this phantom of a chapel illuminated by invisible tapers that burn in the open air, even in snow and wind. You may laugh at it if you like, but a vine-dresser of the place, named Garrigue, doubtless a descendant of Garrigou, declared to me that one Christmas night, when he was a little tipsy, he lost his way on the hill of Trinquelague; and this is what he saw. . . . Till eleven o'clock, nothing. All was silent, motionless, inanimate. Suddenly, about midnight, a chime sounded from the top of the steeple, an old, old chime, which seemed as if it were ten leagues off. Very soon Garrigue saw lights flitting about, and uncertain shadows moving in the road that climbs the hill. They passed on beneath the chapel porch, and murmured:

"Good evening, Master Arnoton!"

"Good evening, good evening, my friends!" . . .

When all had entered, my vine-dresser, who was very courageous, silently approached, and when he looked through the broken door, a singular spectacle met his gaze. All those he had seen pass were seated round the choir, and in the ruined nave, just as if the old seats still existed. Fine ladies in brocade, with lace head-dresses; lords adorned from head to foot; peasants in flowered jackets such as our grandfathers had; all with an old, faded, dusty, tired look. From time to time the night birds, the usual inhabitants of the chapel, who were aroused by all these lights, would come and flit round the tapers, the flames of which rose straight and ill-defined, as if they were burning behind a veil; and what amused Garrigue very much was a certain personage with large steel spectacles, who was ever shaking his tall black wig, in which one of these birds was quite entangled, and kept itself upright by noiselessly flapping its wings. . . .

At the farther end, a little old man of childish figure was on his knees in the middle of the choir, desperately shaking a clapperless and soundless bell, whilst a priest, clad in ancient gold, was coming and going before the altar, reciting prayers of which not a word was heard. . . . Most certainly this was Dom Balaguère in the act of saying his third low mass.

7 | Eugène Sue

This nineteenth-century anti-Jesuit French novelist (1804–1857) is best known for *Les Mystères de Paris* and for *Le Juif errant*. His treatment of *Les Sept péchés capitaux* includes, naturally, a novelette on gluttony—available in English translation (New York: Yurita Press, 2015). Here is an extract:

"A painter or a poet would have made an enchanting picture of this trout with Montpellier butter preserved in ice," said the canon to Pablo. "See there, this charming little trout, with flesh the colour of a rose, and a head like mother-of-pearl, voluptuously lying on this bed of shining green, composed of fresh butter and virgin oil congealed by ice, to which terragon, chive, parsley, and water-cresses have given this bright emerald colour! And what perfume! How the freshness of this seasoning contrasts with the pungency of the spices which relieve it! How delicious! And this wine of Sauterne! As the great man of the kitchen says, how admirably this ambrosia is suited to the character of this divine trout which gives me a growing appetite!" [Culinary Principles 14]

After the trout came another dish, accompanied with this bulletin:

"Fillets of grouse with white Piedmont truffles, minced raw.

"Enclose each mouthful of grouse between two slices of truffle, and moisten the whole well with sauce à la Perigueux, with which black truffles are mingled.

"Masticate *forte,* as the white truffles are raw.

"Drink two glasses of this wine of Château-Margaux 1834,—it also has made a voyage from the Indies. [Culinary Principle 12]

"This wine reveals itself in all its majesty only in the after-taste."

These fillets of grouse, far from appeasing the growing appetite of the canon, excited it to violent hunger, and, in spite of the profound respect which the orders of the great man had inspired in him, he sent Pablo, before another ringing of the bell, in search of a new culinary wonder.

8 | Norman Douglas

During my freshman year at Cornell University, I was chosen to take part in a unique tutorial program headed by several professors in the College of Arts and Sciences (including "Black Max"—Max Black, the great logician). One of the required readings was Douglas's most famous novel, *South Wind* (1917; repr., New York: Modern Library, 1925). A reason for assigning this book was to move the student away from traditional Christianity (Douglas was an inveterate pagan). Fortunately, this reverse evangelism did not work on me, but I appreciated Douglas's fine take on life on the Mediterranean island of Capri. Here is a memorable gastronomical passage from *South Wind*:

* * *

"You are quite right," the Count was saying to Mr Heard. "The ideal cuisine should display an individual character; it should offer a menu judiciously chosen from the kitchen workshops of the most diverse lands and peoples—a menu reflecting the master's alert and fastidious taste. Is there anything better, for instance, than a genuine Turkish pilaff? The Poles and the Spaniards, too, have some notable culinary creations. And if I were able to carry out my ideas on this point I would certainly add to my list of dishes a few of those strange Oriental confections which Mr Keith has successfully taught his Italian chef. There is suggestion about them; they conjure up visions of that rich and glowing East which I would give many years of my remaining life to see."

"And don't you think," he went on, "that we might revive a few of those forgotten recipes of the past? Not their over-spiced entremets, I mean—their gross joints and pas-tries, their swans and peacocks—but those which deal, for example, with the preparation of fresh-water fishes? A pike, to my way of thinking, is a coarse, mud-born crea-ture. But if you will take the trouble, as I once did, to dress a pike according to the complicated instructions of some obsolete cookery-book, you will find him sufficiently pal-atable, by way of a change."

"You would make an excellent chef!"

"It is plain," added Mr Heard, "that the Count does not disdain to practise his skill upon the most ancient and honourable of domestic arts."

"Indeed I don't. I would cook *con amore* if I had leisure and materials. All culinary tasks should be performed with reverential love, don't you think so? To say that a cook must possess the requisite outfit of culinary skill and temperament—that is hardly more than saying that a soldier must appear in uniform. You can have a bad sol-dier in uniform. The true cook must have not only those externals, but a large dose of general worldly experience.

He is the perfect blend, the only perfect blend, of artist and philosopher. He knows his worth: he holds in his palm the happiness of mankind, the welfare of generations yet unborn."

9 | Marcel Rouff

One of the most delightful gastronomical novels of all time is Rouff's *La Vie et la passion de Dodin-Bouffant, gourmet* (1920); English edition titled, *The Passionate Epicure* (Preface by Lawrence Durrell; New York: Modern Library, 2002). Rouff was a professional writer, friend of the celebrated gourmet Curnonsky, and collaborator on *La France Gastronomique*.

I have chosen extracts from the hilarious encounter between Dodin-Bouffant and German Platonic/neo-Hegelian culinary scholar Prof. Dr. Hugo Stumm, who hopelessly confuses philosophical speculation with the culinary arts but who well represents the frightening attempts at "unifying" everything as carried out by Germany during the nineteenth and twentieth centuries.

For those who enjoy this kind of literature and read French, I also recommend Emile Cabanon's *Un roman pour les cuisinières*, ed. Jacques Simonelli (n.p.: Librairie José Corti, 1962) and Henri Lavedan's *Monsieur Gastère* (Paris: Plon, 1927) in the style of a play text.

* * *

[Prof. Dr Stumm:] "I have already written the 1,783 first pages of an essentially hegelio-platonic work, the title of which is *The Metaphysics of Cookery*...

"Only the Idea of Cookery is important. I have devoted my life to proving this, and have now reached the stage when I consume only boiled potatoes and cabbage-water....

"Greed, which shortly after man's appearance on earth vitiated and complicated the simple wish to survive, has everywhere replaced this original need, and today the elaborate cookery of civilized peoples is as different from primitive nourishment as ..."

"As Black Forest meat-balls from artistic gastronomy," growled Bodin-Bouffant, whose blood was coming to the boil. ... [Author's note: *not*, however, to be placed on the level of the wondrous *Schwarzwaldtorte*.]

"Now you know, of course, Herr Doktor, that the whole Universe, with frenzied and painful efforts, tends to co-ordinate its scattered parts and to rebuild itself in Unity, or rather the Unities of the world of Ideas. It is a fact. Everything which gravitates towards simple Unity consequently escapes the strangle-hold of Matter and returns to its Ideal origins. That is why every philosopher must unreservedly approve the traditional policy of our Hohenzollerns who, pursuing the unification of Germany (under their sceptres) throughout the centuries ... then the unification of Europe, and finally that of the world, have established themselves firmly within the logic of metaphysical order.

"But I return to cookery, and it is from the point of view which I have had the honour of outlining to you, that I shall consider the subject. . . .

"The human effort which will extract cookery from the rut of materialism and set it upon the road of the Spirit consists therefore in uprooting this unhealthy diversity and introducing into its disorder and complexity the elements which must bring it back to primitive Unity, to the light of the Idea! Therefore, we must simplify, simplify utterly, reaccustom our faculties of taste to the few rudimentary flavours, protect them from depraving research, from decadent mixtures, offer them ever more normal satisfactions—that is to say cruder ones, and thus plan for the day when cookery, once more only an element of man's vital instinct, will limit itself to maintaining life, to preparing pieces of raw meat as did our ancestors."

"It seems to me," Dodin mumbled between set teeth, "that your compatriots and certain Americans of my acquaintance are well on that road already. . . ."

10 | A. J. Liebling

A. J. Liebling (1904–1963), a quintessential American journalist and writer, had a great love for France and its cuisine. He spent his career largely at the *New Yorker* magazine. The Liebling papers are archived at my alma mater, Cornell University. The following passage is taken from his *Between Meals: An Appetite for Paris* (San Francisco: North Point Press, 1986).

* * *

In the heroic age before the First World War, there were men and women who ate, in addition to a whacking lunch and a glorious dinner, a voluminous *souper* after the theater or the other amusements of the evening. I have known some of the survivors, octogenarians of unblemished appetite and unfailing good humor—spry, wry, and free of the ulcers that come from worrying about a balanced diet—but they have had no emulators in France since the doctors there discovered the existence of the human liver. From that time on, French life has been built to an increasing extent around that organ, and a niggling caution has replaced the old recklessness; the liver was the seat of the Maginot mentality.

One of the last of the great around-the-clock gastronomes of France was Yves Mirande, a small, merry author of farces and musical-comedy books. In 1955, Mirande celebrated his eightieth birthday. . . . In [his] restaurant on the Rue Saint-Augustin, M. Mirande would dazzle his juniors, French and American, by dispatching a lunch of raw Bayonne ham and fresh figs, a hot sausage in crust, spindles of filleted pike in a rich rose *sauce Nantua*, a leg of lamb larded with anchovies, artichokes on a pedestal of foie gras, and four or five kinds of cheese, with a good bottle of Bordeaux and one of champagne, after which he would call for the Armagnac and remind Madame [the Gasconne cook] to have ready for dinner the larks and ortolans she had promised him, with a few *langoustes* and a turbot—and, of course, a fine *civet* made from the *marcassin,* or young wild boar. . . .

"And while I think of it," I once heard him say, "we haven't had any woodcock for days, or truffles baked in the ashes, and the cellar is becoming a disgrace—no more '34s and hardly any '37s. Last week, I had to offer my publisher a bottle that was far too good for him, simply because there was nothing between the insulting and the superlative." [cf. Culinary Principles 12–15]

11 | M. F. K. Fisher and W. H. Auden

M. K. F. Fisher (1908–1992) was one of the very most prolific and important American culinary writers of the twentieth century. I present, after a passage from her *Serve It Forth* (included, with four of her other classics, in *The Art of Eating* [introductions by Clifton Fadiman and James Beard (New York: Macmillan, n.d.)]), a selection from W. H. Auden's review of the Fisher compilation (W. H. Auden, *Forewords and Afterwords,* ed. Edward Mendelson [London: Faber and Faber, 1979]).

W. H. Auden (*The Age of Anxiety*, etc.) was second only to T. S. Eliot as the greatest of twentieth-century Christian poets in the English language. His poem "Law Like Love" introduces the present author's *Jurisprudence: A Book of Readings.*

* * *

Frederick the Great used to make his own coffee, with much to-do and fuss. For water he used champagne. Then, to make the flavor stronger, he stirred in powdered mustard.

Now to me it seems improbable that Frederick truly liked this brew. I suspect him of bravado. Or perhaps he was taste-blind.

Almost all people are born unconscious of the nuances of flavor. Many die so. Some of these unfortunates are physically deformed, and remain all their lives as truly taste-blind as their brother sufferers are blind to colour. Others never taste because they are stupid, or, more often, because they have never been taught to search for differentiations of flavor. [cf. Culinary Principle 1]

They like hot coffee, a fried steak with plenty of salt and pepper and meat sauce upon it, a piece of apple pie and a hunk of cheese. They like the feeling of a full stomach. They resemble those myriad souls who say, "I don't know anything about music, but I love a good rousing military band."

Let the listener to Sousa hear much music. Let him talk to other music-listeners. Let him read about music-makers.

He will discover the strange note of the oboe, recognize the French horn's convolutions. Schubert will sing sweetly in his head, and Beethoven sweep through his heart. Then one day he will cry, "Bach! By God, I can hear him! I can hear!"

That happens to the taste-blind in just some such way. He eats apple pie, good or bad, because he has always eaten it. Then one day he sees a man turn his back upon the cardboard crust and sodden, half-cooked fruit, and eat instead some crisp crackers with his cheese, a crisp apple peeled and sliced ruminatively after the crackers and the yellow cheese. The man looks as if he knew something pleasant, a secret from the taste-blind.

"I believe I'll try that. It is—yes, it is good. I wonder—"

And the man who was taste-blind begins to think about eating. Perhaps he talks a little, or reads. All he really need do is experiment. . . .

He is pleased. He is awakened. At last he can taste, discovering in his own good time what Brillat-Savarin tabulated so methodically as the three sensations: (1) direct, on the tongue; (2) complete, when the food passes over the tongue and is swallowed; and most enjoyable of all (3) reflection—that is, judgment passed by the soul on the impressions which have been transmitted to it by the tongue. [Culinary Principle 20]

Yes, he can taste at last, and life itself has for him more flavour, more zest.

* * *

Cooking is an art and its appreciation, therefore, is governed by the law which applies to all artistic appreciation. Those who have been subjected too long and too exclusively to bad cooking become incapable of recognizing good cooking if and when they encounter it. Nobody can afford to keep a good professional cook any more and, though there are still good restaurants, their prices are geared to people with expense accounts. For most of us, the possibility of eating well depends upon the skill and passion of the amateur cook, and learning the art should now be regarded as essential to an educated man or woman. At Oxford and Cambridge, for example, I should like to see a stove installed in every undergraduate's room and the College dining-halls transformed into supermarkets and liquor-stores. In the meantime, I would recommend all parents (and godparents) to present their children of both sexes on their sixteenth birthday with a copy of *The Art of Eating.* It will not teach them how to cook, but I cannot think of any other reading-matter which is more likely to inspire them with the desire to learn.

12 | Joseph Wechsberg

Joseph Wechsberg (1907–1983), born in what was then Czechoslovakia, immigrated to the United States when the Nazis invaded his homeland; his mother died at Auschwitz. He had a very distinguished career as a journalist and wrote extensively in the fields of music and gastronomy. Probably his most well-known book is *Blue Trout and Black Truffles: The Peregrinations of an Epicure.* Many of his pieces appeared in the *New Yorker* magazine.

Here is a selection from his handsomely illustrated *The Best Things in Life* (London: Weidenfeld and Nicolson, 1964) followed by a culinary account of his time on shipboard—from my signed copy! (*Looking for a Bluebird* [New York: Penguin Books, 1947].)

* * *

In France . . . the philosophy of good eating is considered an abstract science, and good cooking a major art, not only by a minority of connoisseurs, as is true elsewhere, but by the population at large. A nation's eating standards are set not by its most expensive restaurant but by the quality of its home cooking, and French girls are still brought up in the tradition of their *grand'mères,* who wouldn't have dared marry without knowing how to make a good *omelette aux fines herbes* (not easy, because it must be made within a few seconds). The French working man loves his *bifteck* and *frites* as ardently as French epicures between the wars esteemed Fernand Point's *gratin de queues d'écrevisses*. France is the only country on earth that has a whole flock of institutes devoted to the serious study of food and wine, with no commercial strings attached—an *Académie des Gastronomes*, for instance, and an *Académie du Vin de France*. It not only produces a different cheese for every day of the year—more, in fact, since there are now over four hundred different cheeses in France—but also has *maîtres fromagers* and *officiers de bouche du taste-fromage*. In France, the great chefs have never been considered servants—not even exalted servants—as they have always been in other countries (with the exception of ancient Rome and Greece, where they were men of some importance); rather, they have been considered artists, on the level with the country's great musicians, painters, and writers, and a good cut above politicians, generals and millionaires.

* * *

Captain's Dinner

Aboard the passenger liners of the Compagnie Générale Transatlantique, the Captain's Dinner was given on the evening before the ship's arrival in New York or Southampton....

Even on a comparatively small boat, such as our nine-thousand-ton *La Bourdonnais,* where the cuisine was modest compared to the Brillat-Savarinesque standard aboard the *Paris,* the *France,* and the *Ile de France,* the Captain's Dinner was a treat:

Le Caviar Astrakhan
La Bouillabaisse Marseillaise
Les Raviolis Niçoise
La Sole Meunière
La Poularde Ròtie Lafayette
Les Asperges à l'Huile
Les Pommes de Terre Marie
Marrons Glacés—Petits Fours—Pâtisserie
Les Fromages de Savoie
Le Café de Colombie

The stewards did not bother to show the wine card, simply asking the passengers if they preferred Mumm, Cordon Rouge or the more expensive vintages of Charles Heidsieck, Reims, without mentioning the lesser brands.

13 | Hilaire Belloc

This prolific Anglo-French writer (1870–1953) was a strong Catholic believer who collaborated with G. K. Chesterton on a number of publications. (On Chesterton, see my essay "Chesterton the Apologist" in *Christ as Centre and Circumference*.) Like Chesterton, Hilaire Belloc had a fine sense of humor, as is evidenced by the following culinary poem, titled—not surprisingly—"On Food." (It is included in the fine epicurean anthology *The Gourmet's Companion*, ed. Cyril Ray [London: Eyre and Spottiswoode, 1963].)

* * *

Alas! What various tastes in food,
Divide the human brotherhood!
Birds in their little nests agree
With Chinamen, but not with me.
Colonials like their oysters hot,
Their omelettes heavy—I do not.
The French are fond of slugs and frogs,
The Siamese eat puppy-dogs.
The nobles at the brilliant Court
Of Muscovy, consumed a sort
Of candles held and eaten thus,
As though they were asparagus.

The Spaniard, I have heard it said,
Eats garlic, by itself, on bread:
Now just suppose a friend or don
Dropped in for lunch at half-past one
And you were jovially to say,
"Here's bread and garlic! Peg away!"
I doubt that you would gain your end
Or soothe the don, or please the friend
In Italy the traveller notes
With great disgust the flesh of goats
Appearing on the table d'hôtes:
And even this the natives spoil
By frying it in rancid oil.
In Maryland they charge like sin
For nasty stuff called terrapin;
And when they ask you out to dine
At Washington, instead of wine
They give you water from the spring
With lumps of ice for flavouring,
That sometimes kill and always freeze
The high plenipotentiaries.
In Massachusetts all the way
From Boston down to Buzzards Bay
They feed you till you want to die
On rhubarb pie and pumpkin pie,
And when you summon strength to cry,
"What is there else that I can try?"
They stare at you in mild surprise

And serve you other kinds of pies.
And I with these mine eyes have seen
A dreadful stuff called Margarine
Consumed by men in Bethnal Green.
But I myself that here complain
Confess restriction quite in vain.
I feel my native courage fail
To see a Gascon eat a snail;
I dare not ask abroad for tea;
No cannibal can dine with me;
And all the world is torn and rent
By varying views on nutriment
And yet upon the other hand,
De gustibus non disputandum.

14 | Keith Waterhouse

Keith Waterhouse (1929–2009) was an English journalist and playwright with a passion for the correct use of the English language and the appreciation of fine food. The following passage is taken from his little book *The Theory and Practice of Lunch* (London: Michael Joseph, 1986).

* * *

The definitive Sunday family lunch establishment, so far as I'm concerned, is La Favorita in Sorrento [Italy], which is not so much a restaurant as a culinary stadium, arranged in terraces like an indoor vineyard. The reason it is so huge becomes clear as the place begins to fill up after Mass and whole dynasties troop in to settle themselves around tables for ten, twelve, sixteen, twenty—three or four generations of them, wispy matriarchs all in black, family godfathers stubble-chinned and without collar or tie to their serge suits, barrel-chested married sons and plump daughters-in-law in their Sunday best, teenagers in jeans and sneakers, bambinos got up like pageboys and maids of honour, and all so deferential to one another as, in strict order of precedence, they pass around the mineral water and the wine and the olive oil and help their seniors to salad and sample one another's pasta and seafood.

15 | Robert Farrar Capon

Father Capon (1925–2013) was a High Church American Episcopal priest whose culinary publications integrated gastronomy and theology. He says of his beliefs:

> [God in Christ] has taken away the sins of the world—of every last being in it—and he has dropped them down the black hole of Jesus' death. On the cross, he has shut up forever on the subject of guilt: "There is therefore now no condemnation. . . ." But I am not a universalist. . . . I take with utter seriousness everything that Jesus had to say about hell, including the eternal torment that such a foolish non-acceptance of his already-given acceptance must entail. All theologians who hold Scripture to be the Word of God must inevitably include in their work a tractate on hell. But I will not—because Jesus did not—locate hell outside the realm of grace. Grace is forever sovereign, even in Jesus' parables of judgment. (*The Romance of the Word* [Grand Rapids: Eerdmans, 1996])

Culinary activity is often very laborious and fatiguing, and the results are the most perishable among all artistic creations. Here is a typical example of Capon's theological approach to such efforts in a fallen world (from his classic *The Supper of the Lamb: A Culinary Reflection* [repr., New York: Modern Library, 2002]).

* * *

Between the onion and the parsley . . . I shall give the summation of my case for paying attention. Man's real work is to look at the things of the world and to love them for what they are. That is, after all, what God does, and man was not made in God's image for nothing. The fruits of his attention can be seen in all the arts, crafts, and sciences. It can cost him time and effort, but it pays handsomely. If an hour can be spent on one onion, think how much regarding it took on the part of that old Russian who looked at onions and church spires long enough to come up with St. Basil's Cathedral. Or how much curious and loving attention was expended by the first man who looked hard enough at the inside of trees, the entrails of cats, the hind ends of horses, and the juice of pine trees to realize he could turn them all into the first fiddle. No doubt his wife urged him to get up and do something useful. I am sure that he was a stalwart enough lover of things to pay no attention at all to her nagging; but how wonderful it would have been if he had known what we know now about his dawdling. He could have silenced her with the greatest riposte of all time: Don't bother me; I am creating the possibility of the Bach unaccompanied sonatas.

* * *

For a parallel treatment of wine from a theological viewpoint, see the excellent and moving recent work *The Spirituality of Wine* by Lutheran scholar Gisela H. Kreglinger (Grand Rapids, MI: Eerdmans, 2016).

RECIPES ACROSS THE CENTURIES

1 | Greece

I. Then

Archestratus's *The Life of Luxury* is "Europe's oldest cookery book." It is preserved only in fragments, most of them contained in the multivolume *Deipnosophistae* ("Dinner Table Philosophers") of the learned antiquarian Athenaeus of Naucratis (AD 2–3). The Loeb Classical Library edition of Athenaeus in seven volumes gives both the Greek text and an English translation. The importance of banquets and feasts to life in classical Greece cannot be missed in the works of these authors.

As for Archestratus, his culinary fragments have been translated by John Wilkins and Shaun Hill in *Archestratus: The Life of Luxury* (Totnes: Prospect Books, 1994), in which the following reconstructed recipe appears.

MARINATED AND GRILLED MACKEREL (OR TUNA)

Ingredients

For 4 people

4 mackerel or a similar quantity of small Mediterranean tuna

Garum fish sauce, best approximated with 200ml of the Thai/Vietnamese commercial *Nam Pla* sauce—made from fermented fish, salt, and water

2 tablespoons olive oil

Method

Prepare the fish by gutting and scaling it. If you prefer, the fish may be filleted.

Marinate the fish in *Nam Pla* for 2 hours, then lift out and pat dry. Brush with olive oil.

Grill and then serve moistened with a few drops of *Nam Pla* and a salad of bitter leaves.

II. Now

In my view, the most interesting contemporary Greek cuisine is that of Crete. Even if the ancient adage "All Cretans are liars" were true and one could solve the conundrum that has plagued philosophers ("That being the case, could you accept as true that statement if asserted by a Cretan?"), it would have no bearing on the fine cuisine of that Greek island.

The Cretans have the longest lifespans of any Europeans, and they attribute this to their cuisine—*plus* the God of the Bible and of the Orthodox Church, to be sure. When my son and daughter-in-law accompanied my wife and me on a Cretan holiday, we naturally expected it to prolong our lives. (I, myself, however, attribute my longevity first and foremost to fine French wine.)

The following recipe comes from *The Art of Greek Cookery* by the Women of St. Paul's Greek Orthodox Church (Garden City: Doubleday, 1963), a book carrying Craig Claiborne's imprimatur. See also Maria and Nikos Psilakis's *La Cuisine Crétoise* (new ed. [Heraklion: Karmanor, 2000]).

SKALTSOUNIA (CRETAN TURNOVERS)

Ingredients

Turnovers:

½ lb feta cheese

1 3-oz package cream cheese

2 eggs, beaten

2 tablespoons dried mint leaves, crushed

½ cup butter, softened

Pastry dough (see below)

Oil or fat for frying (optional)

Sugar or honey for topping

Pastry:

4 cups flour

½ teaspoon salt

½ cup shortening

½ to 1 cup cold water

Method

Turnovers:

Combine cheese and eggs in a bowl and whip until smooth. Add mint
  and mix in butter. Set aside while making pastry.

Roll out dough on a floured board as thinly as possible. Cut dough into
3-in rounds. Place 1 heaping tablespoon of filling on each round, fold
over dough as in making turnovers, moisten edges, and seal.
If desired, fry in olive oil or hot fat until light brown on both sides.
Place on platter and sprinkle with sugar or dip in honey. Or, if
preferred, turnovers may be placed on an ungreased baking sheet
and baked in a 350° oven for 15 to 20 min or until golden, then
sprinkled with sugar or dipped in honey. Yield: approximately 3 doz.

Pastry:
Sift flour and salt into mixing bowl. Cut in shortening with pastry cutter
or two knives. Stir in enough water to make a firm dough that can be
gathered together.

2 | Rome

I. Then

The pseudonymous author of *Apician Morsels* (London: Whittaker, Treacher, 1829) thus describes Roman eating ideals: "Among the luxuries of the table in greatest request, Gellius quotes out of Varro, the peacock from Samos, the Phygrian turkey, cranes from Melos, Ambracian kids, the Tartesian mullet, trouts from Persenumtium, Tarentine oysters, crabs from Chios, Tatian nuts, Egyptian dates, Iberian chestnuts; all of which institutions of bills of fare were invented for the wicked wantonness of luxury and gluttony."

The latter comment was nicely confirmed in an eighteenth-century introduction to the culinary habits of the Romans, cited by the author of *Apician Morsels* from correspondence between Dr. William King and Dr. Lister and others (included in King's *Art of Cookery: In Imitation of Horace's Art of Poetry* [London: Bernard Lintott, 1708]): "The most exquisite Animal was ... the *Dormouse*, a harmless Creature, whose Innocence must at least have defended it both from Cooks and Physitians."

The aphorism is correct: "When Rome conquered Greece, Greece conquered Rome." The Romans loved their banquets, as did the Greeks. Unhappily, among wealthy Romans, the result was often disgusting excess. Therefore, I have foregone descriptions of recipes from Petronius's account of Trimalchio's feast in the *Satyricon* (not a pleasant memory of my classical studies at Cornell University).

Instead, I offer a recipe from the greatest of all the Roman cookbooks that have come down to us from antiquity, the *Apicius*. *Apicius* is a fourth- or fifth-century AD pseudepigraphal collection of recipes attributed to the first-century gourmet Marcus Gavius Apicius. The great French edition of *Apicius* was prepared by Bertrand Guégan (for whom the chair I occupy at the Académie de Gastronomie Brillat-Savarin is named). The Late Latin text with accompanying English translation is available as *Apicius: The Roman Cookery Book*, translated by Barbara Flower and Elisabeth Rosenbaum (London: Peter Nevill, 1958). On both Greek and Roman gastronomy, I suggest Andrew Dalby and Sally Grainger's lavishly illustrated *Classical Cookbook* (Los Angeles: J. Paul Getty Museum, 1996).

I do not suggest that you hunt the wild boar for the following recipe yourself; they are very dangerous beasts and are nasty even when little. Fascinatingly, in the French language, the words for the edible baby wild boar (*mar-cassin*) and the tough adult wild boar (*sanglier*) have no etymological connection. Conclusion: to a true French-man, whether or not you can eat it is far more important than its biological connections.

> ## BOAR
>
> Sponge it and sprinkle with salt and grilled cumin, and leave it so. The next day, put it in the oven. When it is cooked, pour a hot sauce over it. The sauce: Take pepper, lovage, celery-seed, mint, thyme, toasted pine-kernels, wine, vinegar, *liquamen,* and a little oil. When the liquid in which the boar is roasting has boiled, put the pounded mixture in and stir with a bunch of onions and rue. If you wish to make it thicker, bind the juice with white of eggs, stir slowly, sprinkle with ground pepper, and serve.

II. Now

Italy is a country of great diversity. From the rather serious northern part (Milan, Florence, Siena, Venice), one goes through Rome to the southern regions of the peninsula. The cuisine moves correspondingly from North European sophistication to the lighthearted Southern fare—paralleling the character of the cooks and the public that one meets on the way.

I choose a dish that combines the bourgeois (spaghetti) with the aristocratic (truffles). The recipe can be found in Anna Del Conte's *The Concise Gastronomy of Italy* (New York: Barnes and Noble, 2004). Other excellent works on Italian gastronomy include Luigi Carnacina's *Great Italian Cooking* (New York: Adradale Press, n.d.) and the Italian

Academy of Cookery's *The Italian Cookery Book* (London: Pelham Books, 1986).

SPAGHETTI ALLA NURSINA (SPAGHETTI WITH BLACK TRUFFLES)

Ingredients

Serves 4

2½ oz black truffles (preferably the majestic black truffle of Norcia in Umbria)

7 tablespoons olive oil

1 garlic clove, crushed

2 salted anchovies, boned, rinsed, and chopped or 4 canned or bottled anchovy fillets, drained and chopped

Salt and freshly ground black pepper

12 oz thin spaghetti

Method

Scrub the truffles gently under cold water and then pat them dry with paper towels. Grate the truffles through the smallest holes of a cheese grater.

Put the truffles with half the olive oil in a small saucepan and cook over a very low heat for 1 minute. Take off the heat, add the garlic and anchovies; mash and pound the mixture with a fork.

Return to the heat and cook very gently for a further 5 minutes, stirring the whole time. (The heat must be very low—on no account should the sauce be allowed to boil.) Taste and add salt if necessary, and a generous amount of pepper.

Cook the spaghetti and toss with the remaining olive oil in a heated serving dish; spoon over the truffle sauce. Serve immediately.

3 | Medieval Europe and the Avignon Papacy

The so-called Middle Ages (a term coined during the Renaissance to designate the entire period between classical antiquity and the "modern" time of the Renaissance) covers a vast time span—whether we take its *terminus a quo* as the fall of the Roman Empire or Charlemagne's coronation as Holy Roman Emperor on Christmas Day in the year 800. Culinary activity during those many centuries, like political activity, was essentially regional, and there was a great gulf between humble peasant meals and the feasts of the noble classes and higher clergy.

Fascinatingly, the "highest" of haute cuisine was developed, along with the greatest medieval libraries, at the papal court at Avignon during the so-called Great Schism and Babylonian captivity of the church (1309–1377) when Europe had three popes (Italian, French, and Spanish), all excommunicating each other. The French popes were not strong on theology but were very strong on culture—including, of course, gastronomy. It does not go too far to locate the origins of modern French haute cuisine during that truly awkward period of church history—exported to France especially under the influence of Catherine de Medici, great granddaughter of Lorenzo the Magnificent and wife of French king Henry II.

I include here a fifteenth-century recipe from Harleian MS 279 (*Two Fifteenth-Century Cookery-Books*, ed. Thomas Austin [London: The Early English Text Society by N. Trübner and Co., 1888]). See, in general, Terence Scully's *The Art of Cookery in the Middle Ages* (Woodbridge, Suffolk: Boydell, 1995) and, with special reference to the English Middle Ages, Maggie Black's *The Medieval Cookbook* (London: British Museum Press, 1992).

VENYSON RIBS IN WINE BROTH

Ingredients

Venison ribs
Parsley, chopped
Sage
Black Pepper
Cloves (powder)
Mace
Red Wine Vinegar
Red Wine

Method

Take ribs of venison, and wash them clean in fair water, and strain the same water through a strainer into a pot, and add there-to Venison, also Parsley, Sage, powder pepper, Cloves, Mace, Vinegar, and a little red wine add there-to; and then let it boil until it is done, & serve forth.

4 | Renaissance

It began early in the fourteenth century with Petrarch's ascent of Mont Ventoux just to enjoy the experience (but once at the peak, he read his St. Augustine, demonstrating that in the recovery of the natural creation, the Renaissance man did not forget Christian redemption). It flourished in Florence, Italy, with the likes of Leonardo Da Vinci. It ended in France, when Michelangelo decamped north of the Alps. Or better, it continued among the scholars of the so-called Northern Renaissance, chief of whom was Erasmus, who, it was correctly said, "laid the egg that Luther hatched," by way of his criticism of church corruption and his first printed edition of the Greek New Testament.

Since one of the major themes of the Renaissance was the recovery of classical antiquity, it comes as no surprise that the cuisine of the time drew on classical sources. But in doing so, it did not discard the medieval heritage of fine local dishes.

Here is a recipe related to the life and career of Renaissance Latinist Poggio Bracciolini (1380–1459); it can be found in Gillian Riley's *Renaissance Recipes* (San Francisco: Pomegranate Artbooks, 1993). This dish was enjoyed at Bracciolini's house in Florence by Bartolomeo Platina, the author of the first printed cookbook, his *De honesta voluptate et valitudine* (on Platina as gastronome, see Joseph D. Vehling's *Platina and the Rebirth of Man* [Chicago: Walter M. Hill, 1941]; on Platina as bibliophile, see my work *A Seventeenth Century View of European Libraries*).

CHICKEN WITH VERJUICE, "AMOROSA"

Ingredients

1 medium-sized, free-range chicken, jointed

4 oz (120 gr) *pancetta* or unsmoked fatty bacon

1 lb (500 gr) sour green grapes, gooseberries, or unripe green plums for the verjuice

Fresh mint and parsley, chopped

Salt, freshly ground black pepper, and saffron to taste

Method

Fry the chicken joints and diced bacon in olive oil until golden and half cooked. Crush the sour grapes and strain the juices through a sieve into a casserole. Add the chicken. Stir well to dissolve any brown bits, and simmer until the chicken is tender. Season with pepper and powdered saffron and check for salt (the bacon may have provided enough). Serve sprinkled with the chopped herbs.

5 | Classic French Cuisine

Antonin Carême

The *Larousse Gastronomique* puts it this way: "Carême should be regarded, even today, as the founder of '*la grande cuisine*,' classic French cookery. His theoretical work, his practical work as an inventor of sauces [Culinary Principle 11], as pastrymaker, designer and author of works devoted to cooking, place him at an immense distance from all those who preceded him in his career" (see introduction by A. Escoffier, ed. Prosper Montagné [New York: Crown Publishers, 1965], 214).

Antonin Carême (1784–1833) created magnificent, architecturally designed desserts for the likes of Talleyrand and Napoleon. After the fall of Napoleon, he decamped to England (1816–1817). While there, he suffered the fate of being one of three cooks to the prince regent (the future King George IV)—Carême handling the entrées, another the roasts, and the third the pastry and sweets. Each went his own way without consulting the others. Carême saw this

an unpardonable culinary sin, since it prevented the creation of integrally planned meals (Culinary Principle 19.)
When the prince went to Brighton, he took only Carême
with him; there the chef prepared the lavish menus worthy of his talents. Remarked the prince one day, "Carême,
you will be the death of me; you send in such appetizing
fare that I cannot help overeating." Carême's response
was, "Sir, my duty is to tempt your appetite; yours, to con-
trol it."

After England, Carême spent a brief time in St. Peters-
burg by invitation of Tsar Alexander I, returning to Paris
to become chef to rich banker James Mayer Rothschild.

Carême wrote prolifically on the history and practice of
cuisine. See, for example, his *Le Cuisinier Parisien, ou l'Art
de la cuisine française au XIXe siècle* (2nd ed. [Paris: Firmin
Didot, 1828]). As a secondary source, see Ian Kelly's *Cooking
for Kings: The Life of Antonin Carême* (London: Short Books,
2003), valuable especially for its inclusion of a number of
original Carême recipes.

Since Carême made his name initially as a pastry cook
and was the inventor of the soufflé, I have chosen to
include his archetypal Soufflé Rothschild. Note that his
Patissier pittoresque (4th ed. [Paris: Garnier, 1842]) consists essentially of illustrations of the magnificent dessert
creations for which he became justly famous.

Not so incidentally, the finest soufflés I have eaten have
been served at the Pont de l'Ill restaurant in La Wantzenau, near Strasbourg.

SOUFFLÉ ROTHSCHILD

Prepare a cream-base soufflé mixture to which 2 to 3 tablespoons of candied fruits (a *salpicon*—finely diced fruits bound with a sauce) soaked in brandy have been added.

When the soufflé is almost cooked, decorate with crystallised cherries.

* * *

Because of Carême's service with Talleyrand, I cannot resist including here the following historical Talleyrand story: "On one occasion this Director [Larevellière-Lépaux] read a long paper explaining his religious system to his ministerial colleagues. After most of them had offered their congratulations, the Minister for Foreign Affairs, Talleyrand, remarked: 'For my part, I have only one observation to make. Jesus Christ, in order to found His religion, was crucified and rose again. You should have tried to do something of the kind.'" (Arnold Toynbee, *A Study of History: Abridgment of Vols. I–VI* [Oxford: Oxford University Press, 1987], I, 493–94.)

Alexis Soyer

Alexis Soyer (1809–1858) was a landmark figure in gastronomy (cf. his massive *Pantropheon, or A History of Food and Its Preparation in Ancient Times* [1853; repr., London: Paddington Press, 1977]). Emigrating from France for political reasons, Soyer served as chef to the Reform Club in London, catered for the coronation breakfast of Queen Victoria, and was responsible for the "Universal [Gastronomic] Symposium of All Nationa" at the Great

Exposition of 1851 (on that event, see my book *The Shaping of America*). His invention of a portable "magic stove" was a work of sheer genius and led to the creation of military field stoves.

But the lasting fame of this good-humored culinary dandy rests on his charitable and philanthropic labors to raise the level of ordinary eating on many different fronts. During the Great Famine in Ireland (1845–1852)—when my great-grandfather for whom I am named left the Emerald Isle for the United States—Soyer set up portable soup kitchens to feed the starving. At his own expense, he made military food edible and saved many lives during the Crimean War. There he worked with Florence Nightingale, whose epitaph for him could not be bettered: "Others have studied cookery for the purposes of gormandising (that is, of greed), and others for show, but none but he for the purpose of cooking large quantities of food in the most nutritious manner for large numbers of men. He has no successor" (quoted in Cecil Woodham-Smith, *Florence Nightingale 1820–1910* [London: Penguin Press/Random House, 1955]). Soyer's own account of his Crimean War activities has been reprinted with an introduction by Elizabeth Ray in *A Culinary Campaign* (Lewes: Southover Press, 1995).

On Soyer in general, see Ruth Brandon, *The People's Chef: The Culinary Revolutions of Alexis Soyer* (New London: John Wiley, 2004); Andrew Langley, ed., *The Selected*

Soyer (Bath: Absolute Press and the Reform Club, 1987); Elizabeth Ray, *Alexis Soyer, Cook Extraordinary* (Lewes, East Sussex: Southover Press, 1991); and James A. Beard's introduction in *Soyer's Cookery Book* (New York: David McKay, 1959).

The following recipe is number 33 of Soyer's "Bill of Fare for London Suppers," a kind of appendix to his *A Culinary Campaign*. Soyer writes, "In introducing the subjoined Bill of Fare, applicable to the London suppers, I must here repeat that which I have previously mentioned, that my idea is far from replacing the dishes now so much in vogue both at the 'Albion,' Simpson's in the Strand [where, incidentally, my wife, Lanalee de Kant Montgomery, played harp in the 1990s], Evans's Cider Cellars, and such-like places, but now and then a couple of dishes taken from these receipts cannot fail to prove agreeable to the partakers, without much interfering with the regular routine of the nightly business of such establishments."

STEWED OYSTERS ON TOAST

Open a dozen of oysters, put them in a small stewpan, add to them two grains of black pepper, a little salt, butter, cayenne, and sugar; set on the stove for a few minutes until set—say three or four minutes; having only given them a slight boil, put in a piece of butter as big as a walnut, which you have mixed with half a teaspoonful of flour, shake the stewpan round by the handle, to melt the contents; put it back on the fire just to simmer, and serve on toast. A drop of cream is an improvement. If not enough liquor, add a drop of milk.

Over-stewed oysters are as bad as over-cooked kidneys. For a large quantity, proceed the same. The only thing to be observed is, that the oysters are properly set before serving, they being neither raw nor overdone.

Auguste Escoffier

Auguste Escoffier (1846–1935) was one of the very greatest of modern French chefs, whose reputation was made (remarkably) in London at the Ritz Carlton and the Savoy Hotel. He was known as "the king of chefs and the chef of kings." His classic—and massive—*Ma Cuisine* is available in English (rev. ed. [New York: Bonanza Books, 1984]). See also *The Escoffier Cook Book* (New York: Crown Publishers, 1941); *The Illustrated Escoffier*, ed. Anne Johnson (New York: International Culinary Society/Crown Publishers, 1987); and Joseph Wechsberg's *Red Plush and Black Velvet: The Story of Dame Nellie Melba and Her Times* (London, 1962).

Rather than including here one of Escoffier's grandiose main course recipes, I have chosen the simple *Pêches Melba*. Escoffier named the dish for the celebrated Australian opera singer Nellie Melba.

Nellie Melba often ate at Escoffier's restaurants while performing in Covent Garden during the late 1890s and early 1900s. Nellie sent Escoffier tickets to her performance in the Wagner opera *Lohengrin*. The production featured a beautiful boat in the shape of a swan. The following evening, Escoffier presented Nellie with a dessert of fresh peaches served over vanilla ice cream—in a silver dish perched atop a swan carved from ice. He originally called the dish "Peaches with a Swan." A few years later, when Escoffier opened the Ritz Carlton in London with César Ritz, he changed the dish slightly by adding a topping of sweetened raspberry purée and renaming the dish *Pêches Melba.*

PÊCHES MELBA

If you are not inclined in a peach direction, you can modify this recipe (as restaurants do regularly) to arrive at Fraises Melba, Framboises Melba, *and so on.*

Ingredients

Peaches
Sugar
Vanilla ice cream
Raspberry purée
Sliced "green" almonds [not dried almonds] (optional)

Method

Peel and stone the peaches, and sprinkle with sugar. The peaches should be ripe, dipped into boiling water, then into ice water, and the skins removed.

Put the ice cream in a serving dish or in individual dishes, arrange the peaches on top, and cover with the sweetened purée.

Sprinkle the almonds on top.

6 | The Ottomans

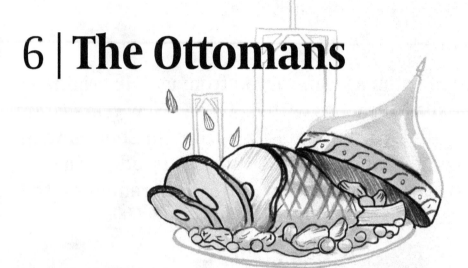

Politically and religiously, Ottoman hegemony does not constitute a happy phase in Western history. The capture of Constantinople by the Ottoman Turks in 1453 ended the eastern Roman Empire and the sway of the Orthodox Church in the Near East. At the time of the Protestant Reformation, Roman Catholic emperor Charles V tried (unsuccessfully, thank heaven) to persuade the early Lutheran princes to give up their beliefs and unite with him to defend against the Turks who were threatening Europe at the gates of Vienna. (They were beaten back, anyway.)

But gastronomically, the Ottomans were surely on the side of the angels. Their recipes have been very hard to reconstruct, particularly in the absence of quantities of particular ingredients. But excellent work has been done by the Asitane restaurant in Istanbul, and that is certainly the place to go to sample genuine Ottoman fare. (My advice is to stay away from the so-called Ottoman restaurants close to the former Orthodox Church of Hagia

Sophia, now transformed into a mosque and museum, since I found them a disappointment.)

The best scholarly publication on the subject (granting its limitations) is Marianna Yerasimos's *500 Years of Ottoman Cuisine* (trans. Sally Bradbrook [Istanbul: Boyut, 2015]), which contains the following fifteenth- or sixteenth-century classic recipe.

MUTANCENE (SWEET-SOUR LAMB)

Ingredients
Serves 4–6

1–1.2 kg mutton on the bone (preferably shoulder), cut into steak-sized chunks.

30 g honey

3 dessert spoons vinegar

200 g fresh black grapes

200 g dried black plums

200 g dried apricots

500 g almonds

4 medium-sized onions

Freshly milled pepper

Salt

Method
Fill the pan with enough water completely to cover the meat, and cook on a medium heat until the meat is tender, or for 1–1.5 hours. Skim off the scum which forms on the surface of the water, and if the level of the water goes down, add some hot water a little at a time.

Remove the stones from the plums and cut them in half. Put them and the apricots in water to soak for 15–20 minutes.

Soak the almonds in hot water for 10 minutes or so, then remove their
skins and cut them into quarters.

Chop the onions finely, or purée them in a blender.

When the meat is tender, take it out of the pan, and set 1–1.5 cups aside.

Put this stock into a clean pan, and bring to a boil. When it begins to
boil, add the chopped, raw onions. Stir them in, then add the meat
and almonds. Add salt, freshly milled pepper and the honey. At this
point, if the meat is not fatty, add 30 g of butter. Put the lid on the
pan, and, stirring every now and again, cook it on a low heat for
20–30 minutes—until the stock begins to reduce.

Without removing the pan from the heat, add the grapes, plums and
apricots. Making sure that the fruit doesn't disintegrate, cook for
another 10 minutes. Add 3 dessert spoons of vinegar so that the
result is not too sweet. "Let it not be overly sweet, not overly sour."

Remove the pan from the heat, put its contents on a serving dish, and
arrange the almonds and the fruit around the edge.

Extra sauce may be served in another bowl.

7 | Chinese Cuisine

Second only to the French in delicacy and sophistication (Culinary Principle 5), Chinese cuisine employs a remarkable combination of flavors to achieve unparalleled gastronomical results (Culinary Principle 10). I have lectured in Beijing on several occasions (including the presentation of human rights lectures!), and my favorite restaurant is the Fangshan 仿膳饭庄, the oldest of Beijing's imperial restaurants, stunningly located in Beihai Park; it is particularly renowned for its fourteen-course (!) "Emperor's Dinner."

One of the greatest modern exponents of Chinese gastronomy was Kenneth Lo (1938–1995), whose autobiography is "must" reading: *The Feast of My Life* (London: Doubleday, 1993). The following recipe is contained in Lo's *Classic Chinese Cuisine* (London: Simon and Schuster, 1992).

LUO BO MEN NIU NAN (RED-COOKED FIVE SPICE BEEF WITH TURNIP)

Ingredients (for 6–7 portions)

1.25 kg (2½ lb) shin beef

500 g (1 lb) turnips

3½ tablespoons vegetable oil

2 medium onions, thinly sliced

3 slices root ginger, shredded

¾ teaspoon five spice powder

Salt, to taste

900 ml (1½ pint) water

3½ tablespoons dark soya sauce

2 teaspoons sugar

6 tablespoons rice wine or dry sherry

Method

Boil beef for 10 minutes and cut into 4 x 2.5 cm (1½ x 1 inch) cubes. Clean and cut turnips diagonally into 4 cm (1½ inch) pieces.

Heat oil in a casserole or heavy pan. When hot, add beef and stir-fry the beef cubes for 3–4 minutes. Remove with perforated spoon and set aside.

Add onions, ginger, five spice and salt. Stir-fry for 3–4 minutes. Pour in water. Add soya sauce, sugar, wine or sherry. Bring contents to a boil. Add the beef cubes. When contents return to the boil, reduce heat to a minimum, cover and simmer very gently for 1½ hours. Add the turnips and turn the contents over several times. Add 300 ml (½ pint) of water if the contents begin to run too dry. Turn the contents over again. Cover the casserole and place in an oven preheated to 195°C (390°F/Gas mark 6) for a further 1¾ hours.

Serve over rice.

8 | Eating Hungarian

Hungarian cuisine is often disregarded—to the great loss of the gourmet. Hungarian dishes (and wines) deserve far more attention than they normally receive.

As for wines, the Tokay is preeminent. Fascinatingly, the Alsatian *pinot gris* used to be designated also as a Tokay—until the Hungarian wine producers put a stop to that by legal action. In my book *The Transcendent Holmes*, I suggested that Holmes drank the Alsatian Tokay—to the horror of the distinguished Sherlockian who wrote the preface.

The book on the subject, with a preface by Joseph Wechsberg, is the *Cuisine of Hungary* by George Lang, the owner of the wonderful Gundel restaurant in Budapest (as well as the Café des Artistes in New York City). Go to the Gundel for an unforgettable meal with background entertainment by Hungarian gypsy musicians, of course. The following recipe appears in Lang's book (2nd ed. [New York: Wings Books/Random House, 1994]).

BORJÚPÖRKÖLT (DRY-STEWED VEAL)

Ingredients

2 lbs young veal, cut from the leg or leaner part of the breast and shoulder

2 tablespoons lard (amount depends on fattiness of the meat)

1 large onion, minced

1 heaping tablespoon of paprika

1 garlic clove, chopped and mashed (optional)

1 scant teaspoon salt

1 medium-sized, very ripe tomato, or 2 drained, canned Italian tomatoes

1 green pepper, cored and diced

Method

Cut the veal into 1-in dice.

Melt the lard in a heavy stewing casserole or Dutch oven and fry onion until it is light brown.

Remove from heat and mix in the paprika, garlic (if used), salt and veal. Cover, and start cooking over a very low heat.

The simple but tricky secret of this dish is to let the meat cook in the steam from its own juices and the juices of the onion.

Just before the stew starts burning, add a few tablespoons of water; repeat this during the first 10 minutes of cooking whenever liquid evaporates.

Meantime, blanch tomato, peel, and dice.

When the meat is beginning to get soft, in 10 to 15 minutes, add tomato and green pepper. Cook for another 10 to 20 minutes, depending on the age of the veal. Continue to add water bit by bit whenever the moisture evaporates.

When the meat is done, let the liquid reduce as much as possible without burning it. At that point, you should have a rich, dark, red and gold sauce/gravy, neither too thin nor too heavy. The texture must be achieved without any thickening.

Note that the meat must be cooked just as the last of the liquid is evaporated, so that the meat is "singed" in the last few minutes.

Serve with little dumplings.

9 | America—Then and Now

I. Early Times

One can hardly praise the most influential Founding Fathers for their eighteenth-century "Enlightenment" deism or for their social policies (e.g., toleration of slavery). However, particularly because of the shared ideals of American and French revolutionaries, they and their new nation accepted and benefited greatly from culinary influences from the other side of the Atlantic. One thinks of Jefferson at Monticello and Franklin's time as minister plenipotentiary (ambassador) to France. (On the ideological background, see my work *The Shaping of America*.)

Martha Washington had a well-deserved reputation as a fine cook. I provide here one of her recipes from her manuscript cookbook, edited with notes by Karen Hess: *Martha Washington's Booke of Cookery* (New York: Columbia University Press, 1995). See also Stephen A. McLeod, ed., *Dining with the Washingtons* (Chapel Hill: University of North Carolina Press, n.d.), and cf. Amelia Simmons,

The First American Cookbook: A Facsimile of "American Cookery," 1796 (New York: Dover, 1984).

> ### ROAST CAPON WITH OYSTERS
>
> Take a fat Capon & pull [i.e., pluck] & draw it. Then stuff the body with raw oysters. Then truss & lay it to the fire, & set a clean dish under it to save the gravie. Then make the sauce for it, with water that cometh from the oysters, & a little claret, a little pepper & vinegar & the gravie, & rub an ounion up & downe the sauce that it may taste well of it. When it hath boyled a little, put in some butter and mince in some leamon and leamon pill [peel]. Then serve it up with slyced leamon on the capon & round about the dish.

II. Today

There are a host of culinary styles on the American scene, due in large part to the many immigrant cultures that have joined to form the American nation. One could start with Boston baked beans and end with Tex-Mex. I shall not, however, make any attempt to cover this vast gastronomical territory.

By personal choice—particularly since my wife, Lanalee de Kant Montgomery, served for many years as principal harpist of the New Orleans Symphony Orchestra—I provide a recipe from New Orleans. This is typical fare at one of the very best restaurants there: Brennan's. See Deirdre Stanforth, ed., *Brennan's New Orleans Cookbook* (Gretna, LA: Pelican, 1995).

Other possibilities would have been to offer dishes from the Commander's Palace or one of Paul Prudhomme's creations (as described, for example, in his *Chef Paul*

Prudhomme's Louisiana Kitchen [New York: William Morrow, 1984]). The great temptation to do the latter was fueled by Dom DeLuise's Italianish cookbooks (*Eat This... It Will Make You Feel Better* and *Eat This Too!* published by Pocket Books, New York, in 1988 and 1997; videocassettes available). DeLuise successfully impersonated Prudhomme at the latter's own restaurant, since the two looked very much alike and wore similar beards!

SHRIMP CREOLE

Ingredients

4 to 6 servings

½ cup vegetable oil

1 cup coarsely chopped green pepper

2 cups coarsely chopped onion

1 cup chopped celery

2 teaspoons minced garlic

2 cups whole tomatoes

1 tablespoon paprika

¼ tablespoon cayenne

1 teaspoon salt

3 cups water

1 bay leaf

3 lbs raw shrimp, peeled and veined

2 tablespoons cornstarch

Method

Heat vegetable oil and sauté next 4 ingredients until tender. Add tomatoes and brown. Stir in paprika, cayenne, salt and water. Add bay leaf and simmer 15 minutes. Add shrimp and continue simmering 10 to 12 minutes more. If desired, thicken sauce with cornstarch mixed in a little cold water. Serve with hot fluffy rice.

4 Recipes from Today's French Kitchens

1 | Raymond Oliver

Raymond Oliver (1909–1990) was the most famous member of a distinguished culinary family. Oliver's father, Louis, was chef of London's Savoy Hotel, and his son Michel is the author, *inter alia*, of three wonderful children's cookbooks—*La Cuisine est / Les Hors d'oeuvre sont / La Pâtisserie est un jeu d'enfants*. Oliver was well known to a generation of French not because he was owner and chef at the historic three-star Grand Véfour restaurant in Paris but because of his engaging culinary television broadcasts. His comprehensive encyclopedia, *La Cuisine*, has been translated into English by Nika Standen Hazelton and Jack Van Bibber (New York: Leon Amiel, 1969) and is the very best of all such modern treatments—not least (1) because it contains detailed photographs of each basic culinary operation and (2) because the author detests *la nouvelle cuisine* (definition: a very small amount of food on a large, decorated plate—see Culinary Principle 8). Do not go into your kitchen without Oliver's *La Cuisine*! By the way, Oliver's *The French at Table* is also available in English (trans. Claude Durrell [London: Wine and Food Society/Michael Joseph, 1967]).

PINTADEAU TRUFFÉ
(ROAST GUINEA HEN WITH TRUFFLE STUFFING)

Ingredients (for 2 persons)

6 tablespoons butter

3 slices of bacon, diced and blanched

1 shallot, minced

¼ cup uncooked rice

¼ cup *foie gras*, diced

2 truffles, diced

1 guinea hen (2 lbs)

1 tablespoon peanut oil

Salt

Black pepper, freshly ground

Method

Heat 1 tablespoon of the butter in a casserole, add the bacon, the minced shallot, and the rice. Mix and cook, stirring constantly, until the rice is opaque, 3 to 5 minutes.

Add ⅓ cup of water and simmer, covered, for 15 minutes. Remove the casserole from the heat and add the *foie gras* and the truffles.

Stuff the bird with this preparation, sew it closed, and truss it. Heat the oil and the remaining butter in a casserole, and brown the guinea hen on all sides. Season it with salt and pepper.

Transfer the casserole to a preheated 375°F oven and cook, covered, for about 45 minutes.

2 | Paul Bocuse

The reigning emperor of French cuisine was Paul Bocuse, who died at an advanced age in 2018. Here is a simple but enticing recipe from his book for the non-professional cook (*Paul Bocuse in Your Kitchen: An Introduction to Classic French Cooking*, trans. Philip and Mary Hyman [New York: Pantheon Books, 1982]). Bocuse's *magnum opus* is titled *Paul Bocuse's French Cooking.* These titles suggest a rather vain fellow, but having dined at his three-star Lyon restaurant and conversed at length with him some years ago, I can assure the reader that he was not.

FAISAN AUX MARRONS (PHEASANT WITH CHESTNUTS)

Ingredients (3 to 4 servings)

2 ¼ pounds (1 kg) chestnuts

3 to 4 thin slices bacon or salt pork

A pheasant weighing 2 to 2 ½ lbs (900 gr to 1.15 kg) prepared for roasting

2 tablespoons (30 gr) butter—for the bird

Salt

Pepper

4½ tablespoons (70 gr) butter—for the chestnuts

4 tablespoons (6 cl) hot water

1 truffle, finely chopped (optional)

Method

Begin by preparing the chestnuts: since peeling them takes quite a
while, you might plan to do that the day before cooking.

All chestnuts have two skins, a hard outer one and a thin, furry inner one
that clings to the nut. To remove the hard outer one, make a slit in it
with a sharp knife, then peel it off (be careful not to cut the chestnut
in half when making the slit). Place the peeled chestnuts in a large
saucepan, add enough water to cover, a little salt, then cover the pot
and bring to a boil. Boil 5 minutes, then remove the pot from the heat
but leave the chestnuts in the hot water. With a slotted spoon,
remove the chestnuts from the water 3 or 4 at a time, and rub or peel
off the inner skin using a clean cloth or dish towel (this must be done
while the nuts are very hot). Leave the peeled chestnuts
to cool, then place them in a container, close tightly, and put them in
the refrigerator over night—or use them right away if peeling them the
same day you cook the bird.

Attach the slices of bacon or salt pork to the bird, using string or
toothpicks to hold them in place.

Melt 2 tablespoons (30 gr) of butter in a pot large enough to hold the
bird comfortably. Salt and pepper the bird, then brown in the butter
over moderate heat for 10 minutes, turning frequently to brown
evenly. (If the butter blackens, pour it off, wipe the pot clean, and
replace it with new butter.) Butter a piece of parchment paper slightly
larger than the pot, place it over the pot buttered side down, then
cover the pot and cook about 40 minutes more, turning the bird once
or twice.

Just before the bird has finished cooking, melt the remaining
4½ tablespoons (70 gr) butter in a high-sided frying pan and sauté the
chestnuts for 10 minutes, gently shaking the pan frequently to

roll them around in the butter and brown on all sides. Sprinkle with
salt and pepper.

Either serve the bird whole or carve it, placing it on a hot serving platter
surrounded by the chestnuts. Add the hot water to the pot the bird
cooked in, bring just to a boil, season with salt and pepper, and serve
in a sauce boat on the side.

One truffle, finely chopped, can be added to the sauce just before
serving.

3 | Lasserre

LASSERRE

If you can go to only one Parisian restaurant, it simply *must* be Lasserre, on the Avenue Franklin Roosevelt. Yes, it has only two Michelin stars, not three, but the reason appears to be that the restaurant refuses to engage in "innovation"—it has always stood, and continues to stand, for classic French cuisine. My son and I are members of the restaurant's Club des casseroles, which provides *inter alia* a complimentary glass of champagne as an *apéritif.* The roof of the restaurant opens and closes electronically when the weather permits—Lasserre's only concession to modernity.

For the restaurant's history and a selection of its recipes, see Paul Bocuse's preface to Jean-Claude Ribaut's *Lasserre* (Lausanne: Editions Favre, 2007). My recipe here—for one of Lasserre's flagship dishes—benefited also from the *Larousse Gastronomique.*

CANARD À L'ORANGE
(DUCK WITH ORANGE SAUCE)

For 2 people

In a roasting pan, sauté duck until it is brown and roast in oven for
2 hours—or until cooked.

Take it from the oven and flambé it with ½ cup of Grand Marnier. Return
to oven and let it cook for a further 5 minutes.

Drain sauce into a saucepan, adding 1 teaspoon of wine vinegar, same
amount of castor sugar, the juice of 3 oranges, and ½ cup of apricot
liqueur (if not available, add more Grand Marnier).

Peel 3 oranges down to the flesh (definitely no pith) removing all seeds.
Place them in a frying pan, add enough sauce to moisten, and heat
without boiling.

Carve duck, arrange on a warm dish, and surround with slices of
orange. Cover with a suitable quantity of sauce, serving the rest in a
sauceboat.

4 | Le France

No, that is not a misprint for "la France." American and English ships are feminine; French ships are masculine. I am referring to the late, much lamented transatlantic French Line vessel, christened by Yvonne de Gaulle, the president's wife, in 1960 and broken up in 2008. I had the privilege of sailing twice on Le France, once in returning to the United States after obtaining the *Doctorat d'Université* in Protestant theology at the University of Strasbourg and the second time with my son and daughter-in-law on virtually the last voyage of that wondrous ship.

Needless to say, the cuisine on board was magnificent beyond description. Here is a recipe from the book by "the most revered and truly fabled of the French Line's chefs," Henri Le Huédé, *Dining on the France* (New York: Vendome Press, 1981). I have chosen a Normandy dish, reminding the reader of the Norman origins of the Montgomery family (see my autobiography, *Fighting the Good Fight*). Prepare the recipe while drinking a glass of calvados.

DÉLICES DE SOLE
HONFLEURAISE ÉTUVÉS NORMANDE
(SOLE WITH OYSTER SAUCE)

Ingredients

6 filets of sole (about 3 lbs weight)

Salt

5 cups fish stock

4 slices firm white bread

¼ cup (4 tablespoons) clarified butter

For the sauce:

½ cup (8 tablespoons) butter

½ cup flour

2 dozen oysters, shucked

12 stems from large mushrooms, minced

6 egg yolks

⅔ cup *crème fraîche* (or heavy cream)

Method

Wash the filets. Melt butter for sauce in a saucepan and stir in flour. Cook this roux over gentle heat for several minutes without letting it brown. While beating briskly with the whisk, slowly add 2½ cups stock. Bring to a boil, reduce heat, and simmer for 20 minutes. Pass the sauce through a fine sieve and set aside.

Fold fish filets in half and put in a well-buttered pan. Salt lightly and add remaining stock. Poach fish for about 10 minutes, then drain and keep warm.

While fish is poaching, put oysters in a small saucepan with their juices. In another saucepan, mix sauce and minced mushroom stems. Salt lightly, bring to a boil, and simmer for 10 minutes. Strain, adding sauce to oysters. Heat to boiling.

Cut about a dozen *croûtons* from the bread in the shape of an *N* and brown them in clarified butter.

Mix egg yolks and *crème fraîche*. Beat a cup of the hot sauce into the
egg mixture, return the sauce, and simmer, without boiling, until
thickened. Season to taste with salt.

Arrange sole on a platter, overlapping the filets. Cover with the sauce
and arrange the *croûtons* around the edges.

5 | Le Crocodile

It is a sad story. The Crocodile, once Strasbourg's preeminent three-star restaurant, is still there, but it is a shadow of its former self. Emile Jung, owner and chef, retired after the restaurant lost its Michelin rating. Why? Hard to say, though severe published criticisms of the Michelin operation have recently appeared—for example, see a review by Gilles Pudlowski, the editor of a French guide to restaurants considerably more comprehensive and helpful than Michelin's. A "sulfurous" exposé of the Michelin red restaurant guides by Jean-Claude Ribaut is appropriately titled *Rouge de honte* (Gallardon: Menu Fretin, 2011).

Jung well deserved his three-star rating, and I say this not just because he nominated me for membership in the culinary group Club Prosper Montagné. Two books of Le Crocodile recipes exist: Philippe Bohrer's *Au Crocodile* (Paris: Editions Chêne/Hachette, 2012) and Jung's own *À la Table du Crocodile* (Strasbourg: La Nuée Bleue, 2001). I have translated the recipe below from the latter. It is a dessert treat with an Alsatian twist, exemplifying the importance of contrasting but complementary flavors (Culinary Principle 10;

incidentally, since Muenster is a very strong cheese, I advise *all* the diners to choose this dessert; anyone who does not will be overcome by the breath of the other diners).

POIRE ET RAISINS AU MUNSTER EN BIGARADE (PEAR AND GRAPES WITH MUENSTER CHEESE, TART-ORANGE STYLE)

Ingredients

For 4 persons

160 gr Muenster cheese

6 sliced half pears

40 gr dry white grapes

8 cl white wine

40 gr sugar

60 gr vinegar

Salt

Pepper

Parsley leaves

Method

Cut the half pears so as to obtain 12 quarters. Soak the dry grapes in white wine and bring them to a boil so that they swell up. Put the sugar in a small casserole dish with two spoonfuls of water. Let it cook until the water evaporates and the sugar is allowed to caramelize. Carefully add the vinegar to stop the process and dissolve the caramelized sugar. If the sauce is too thick, add two spoonfuls of water.

Cut the Muenster into 12 small slices. Arrange the slices of Muenster and the pear quarters on a plate and heat them in the oven at 180°C for 4 minutes. Lightly salt and pepper the sauce, and pour it over the Muenster and the hot pears. Decorate with some parsley leaves.

Suggested wine: Gewürztraminer *grand cru*.

6 | L'Auberge de l'Ill

This family restaurant is located well off the beaten tourist route (Illhausern, between Strasbourg and Colmar) but is one of the culinary treasures of France. It retained its three-star Michelin rating from 1967 until 2019, surpassed in three-starred longevity only by Paul Bocuse's restaurant in Lyon. (The reduction of the restaurant to two-stars is, not to put too fine a point on it, incomprehensible.) The Auberge de l'Ill features classic French cuisine with special appreciation for Alsatian dishes, and its archetypal recipes, such as saumon soufflé, have not changed in forty years. One restaurant critic has described that dish as "a rectangle of salmon fillet beneath a fluffy overcoat of beaten egg whites flavoured with pike and nutmeg, in a cream and Riesling sauce so rich it would probably be illegal in certain more puritanical countries." (That recipe is available in Paul and Jean-Pierre Haeberlin, *Les Recettes de l'Auberge de l'Ill* [Paris: Flammarion, 1982].)

I have translated a more bourgeois but superb Alsatian recipe from Marc Haeberlin's *L'Alsace Gourmande* (Paris: Albin Michel, 1995), since Haeberlin states, before giving the recipe, "To succeed with this recipe, it is indispensable to obtain the famous Soufflenheim baked-clay terrine, especially created for this dish." The celebrated pottery village of Soufflenheim is where we Montgomerys live, between Strasbourg and the German border, not far from our son's pad in the even smaller village of Nierderrodern.

And I shall not forget a drive many years ago from Strasbourg to Illhausern with my young daughter Catherine in my 1925 Citroën C3 two-seater *décapotable* (convertible) with the top down. She warned me not to take a shortcut; I would not listen, and we found ourselves in a farmer's field with the automatic sprinkler system in full operation. But a little moisture was worth the wonderful lunch at the Auberge de l'Ill.

BAECKEOFFE

Ingredients

For 8 to 10 people

400 gr lamb shoulder, deboned and degreased

400 gr neck of pork, deboned and degreased

400 gr shoulder of beef

3 pig's tails

2 pig's feet

1.5 kg primura potatoes

4 leeks

1 bottle of Alsatian Riesling wine

1 garlic clove

3 large onions

Parsley stems

1 sprig of thyme
1 bay leaf
25 gr butter
Salt
Pepper

For handling the terrine:
200 gr flour
4 soup spoons of cooking oil

Method

Peel the onions and thinly slice them. Cut the several meats into pieces
of 3–4 cm square and put them into a large salad bowl with the
onions, the garlic clove (completely peeled), the thyme, the bay leaf,
and the parsley stems. Apply salt and pepper; pour on the wine. Mix
everything and let it marinate overnight.

Next day, heat your oven to 175°C (thermostat 5). Peel the potatoes,
wash them, and cut them into slices 3–4 mm thick. Season them
with salt and pepper. Wash the leeks and slice them into respectably
sized chunks.

Arrange the terrine in alternating layers: potatoes followed by leeks and
meats mixed together and drained. Continue with this, finishing off
with the potatoes that must be packed firmly down.

Prepare the coating for the terrine: mix the flour and the oil, adding a
little water so as to obtain a supple and homogeneous paste.
Cover the entire surface of the terrine; then place its cover on it,
after having buttered the interior, pressing with sufficient force to
make the paste stick.

Slide the terrine into the oven and let it cook for four hours.

When the Baeckeoffe is ready, bring it to the table in its terrine. Serve it
hot with a seasonal salad.

7 | Le Pont de l'Ill

Drive from Strasbourg to the nearby picturesque town of La Wantzenau (noting a fixed radar limited to seventy kilometers just after an ancient bunker of the Maginot line). You will find this restaurant on the banks of the Ill River, and there you will have a culinary experience second to none. It is a family restaurant, directed by Chef Paul Daull, and—thank heaven—it does not have a Michelin rating, or the prices would be astronomical. It features seafood and shellfish, but there are meat dishes galore for those who prefer them. The fish comes fresh from Brittany and Normandy, and during the winter months, you will meet the bearded fish specialist, replete with tales from his fascinating past. As for dessert, do not depart without having consumed the restaurant's glorious soufflé.

Here is a recipe for the wondrous Brittany lobster served at the Pont de l'Ill from its lobster tank, where your lobster will be introduced to you personally before it is sent to lobster heaven. (From time to time, Normandy lobster is substituted. Are they thinking of the Norman Montgomerys?) I suggest preceding the lobster as a main course (*le plat*) with, as *entrée*, the restaurant's unforgettable fish soup—*Soupe de poisson, avec rouille.*

HOMARD BRETON SAUCE BEURRE BLANC (GRILLED BRITTANY LOBSTER WITH BEURRE BLANC SAUCE)

Ingredients

For 8 persons

The grilled lobster:
8 lobsters (1 per diner)
Olive oil
2 cl whisky

The beurre blanc sauce:
20 cl white wine vinegar
10 cl cream
5 cl sherry vinegar
1 juice of a pressed lemon
500 gr white butter
Fine salt

Method

The grilled lobster:
Remove the claws and the joints, cooking them in boiling water for 15 minutes, then shelling them with the aid of scissors.
Split the body of the lobster in two lengthwise, grilling it in a skillet, flesh side up, with very hot olive oil.
Turn the pieces over and transfer them to an oven plate. Complete the cooking process at an oven temperature of 200°C for about 3 minutes.
When the cooking is finished, flame the lobster with the whisky.

Crack the claws so that the flesh in the claws can be easily removed.

The beurre blanc sauce:

Do a very slow reduction of the white wine vinegar until only about 3 cl remains; at that point, stop the reduction.

Add the cream, the lemon juice, and the sherry vinegar; bring to a boil.

Reduce the heat to moderately low.

Progressively incorporate the softened butter, cutting it into little cubes and whisking it constantly. Mix the white butter using a blender.

Serve the *beurre blanc* right away so that the bites of lobster can be dipped in it.

Appendix A

A Vinific Critique of Bad Biblical Criticism

Let us suppose that a second-century non-Vulgate Latin version of the wedding of Cana pericope in John 2 is discovered in the ruins of an Egyptian monastery. This manuscript has the words for "wine" (*vinum*) and "water" (*aqua*) reversed throughout, so that Jesus changes wine into water. This reading also occurs once in Irenaeus and once in Origen and is employed in an antidrunkenness sermon of the fourth-century ascetic A. Teetotalus.

Dr. C. R. I. ("Carry") Nation is a prominent textual critic of the thoroughgoing eclectic persuasion. From Dr. Nation's literary standpoint, the acceptance of the Latin reading—doubtless derived from a now lost early Greek text of the Gospel—would far better fit the New Testament concern to reduce inebriation (e.g., "Be not drunk with wine, wherein is excess; but be filled with the Spirit"—Eph. 5:18). And it is much earlier than the baseline Greek MSS Codex Sinaiticus and Codex Vaticanus (early to mid-fourth century).

As a result of his internal analysis, Dr. Nation opts for the Latin reading as best fitting the literary context and theology of the Gospel—even though there is almost uniform agreement among the best texts against it.

Dr. Nation has followed the underlying principle of thoroughgoing eclecticism: he has allowed internal literary considerations to trump objective external manuscript evidence.

In spite of his being highly praised by the Baptist and independent fundamentalist churches, which have always been uncomfortable with the historical fact that Jesus turned water into fermented wine, *Dr. Nation should be locked up for his own good and for the good of the church.*

L'ESCARGOT

C'est toi, cher escargot, que je veux célébrer,
Mollusque délectable, honneur de la Bourgogne;
Quand le four t'a doré, je le dis sans vergogne,
Des cupules d'argent j'aime à te retirer.

Le beurre, un peu jaunet, te sied, et c'est merveille
Que ton parfum discret d'ail et persil haché;
On est de bonne humeur après t'avoir mâché
Et l'on trouve divin le fond de la bouteille.[1]

---

1 Gautron du Coudray, *Un quarteron de rimes culinaires* (Le Coteau, France: Editions Horvath, 1985), 18.

Appendix B

Preferences—from the Author's Autobiography

	PLUS	MINUS
Restaurants	Pont de l'Ill (Strasbourg/La Wantzenau) Lasserre (Paris)[1] Rules (London) Fangshan (Beihai Park, Beijing)	All Döner Kebab take-aways and all vegan operations
Foods	Tournedos Rossini, escargots, cuisses de grenouilles à la persillade, crêpes Suzette, virtually anything with caviar or black truffles.	Egg rolls[2], anything containing buckwheat flour or pistachio nuts[3], falafel, merguez (or any other North African dish)
Wines: red	The great French Bordeaux reds, as listed in the 1855 classification	Anything with a Baron de Rothschild label
Wines: white	Pouilly fumé (Dry) Alsatian whites	(Sweet) German/Mosel whites
Wines: sparkling	French crémants, Especially Crémant d'Alsace	All vins mousseux, all pretentious champagnes

[1] My son and I are members of their Club des casseroles.
[2] For which a recipe is given in my *Shaping of America*.
[3] I am deathly allergic to these two items for no known reason. "The whole creation groaneth and travaileth in pain together" (Rom. 8:22).

INDEX OF NAMES

Subject Index

John Warwick Montgomery is well known as a theological writer and as an international trial lawyer (the latter creating a historical bond with magistrate Brillat-Savarin). But he is also learned in gastronomy, as this book evidences, drawing on his vast library of rare culinary classics. He was named one of the fifty living members of the French Académie de Gastronomie Brillat-Savarin (chair 41, Bertrand Guégan). He holds the rank of commander in the international culinary society the Chaîne des Rôtisseurs. On the basis of blind taste tests, he has attained the highest level (*maître*) in the Alsatian wine society, the Confrérie Saint-Étienne. He is also an active member of the Club Prosper Montagné. Professor Montgomery lives in France and England and lectures frequently in the United States.

CPSIA information can be obtained
at www.ICGtesting.com
Printed in the USA
BVHW010316200322
631559BV00004B/5